The Practical Guide to

Career Opportunities in Real Estate

A Survey of Over 35 Careers

with a Focus on

Becoming an Excellent Real Estate Agent

With Introduction to Property Management, Real Estate Finance, Auctions, Leasing, Investing and 1031 Exchange

Copyright © 2021

David Gadish – All Rights Reserved

This book may not be reproduced without the written permission of the author and publisher.

Printed in the United States of America

ISBN: 978-1-954713-00-0

BH4 Publishing

This book is dedicated to my wife, children, and parents.

Motivation

Many people study for, pass their state's real estate exam, and receive their real estate licenses. They start their real estate careers, thinking great success will come quickly. It does not. They get disappointed. Some move from one brokerage to another, possibly again and again, assuming the grass is greener on the other side. Many give up and let their real estate licenses expire.

Multiple studies have shown that 80-90% of those who receive their licenses quit the business within one to two years. This does not need to happen to you.

This book is written for you if you:

- Are interested to learn about the wide range of career opportunities in real estate.
- Wish to enter the real estate field, but not sure in which capacity.
- Are thinking about getting a real estate license but not sure.
- Are studying for your real estate license and want to start planning your next steps.
- Just received your license and not sure where to go next.
- Are looking to join a brokerage, but not sure which one.
- Joined a brokerage in the past year, but it seems like it may not be the right fit.
- Are not sure if to pursue residential real estate, commercial real estate, or both.
- Are not sure if to focus on buyers or sellers.
- Are considering getting a college degree related to real estate but not sure.
- Decided that real estate sales are not for you, but you like real estate and want to pursue a different career in the field.

It is also for you if you gave real estate a try and are about to quit. Do not leave just yet! Read the book and see if a modified strategy could fit you better.

This book will provide you with an understanding of your different options in the real estate industry, both in real estate sales and beyond real estate sales.

Overview

This book is comprised of four parts. Part one provides an introduction to real estate and surveys tens of career paths in the industry. Part two is focused on the most popular career path: real estate sales. Part three looks at what it takes to succeed in real estate sales. Finally, part four looks at a few additional real estate career paths in more detail.

Part One – Introduction to the Real Estate Industry

Part one of the book provides an overview of real estate and real estate careers. Chapter 1 introduces the basics of real estate as well as of the real estate industry. Chapter 2 looks at the different types of residential as well as commercial real estate. Chapter 3 provides a survey of 35 real estate and related careers.

Part Two – Introduction to Real Estate Sales

Part two looks at what successful real estate agents do, from establishing property values to closing deals. Chapter 4 looks at valuation (pricing) of real estate. Chapter 5 looks at how agents handle occupied properties they list for sale. Chapter 6 looks at how agents handle vacant properties. Chapter 7 looks at what agents do to market properties. Chapter 8 looks at how agents manage offers. Chapter 9 looks at how agents handle closings (escrow).

This part of the book is laden with technical details and procedures. They are provided to you so you can determine if real estate sales are genuinely for you. If you find the particulars manageable and of interest to you, then you can use this portion of the book as a reference guide as you pursue this career. Much of the discussion in this part of the book is based on California real estate law and may or may not apply in your state.

Part Three – What It Takes to Succeed in Real Estate Sales

Part three looks at what it takes to be a successful real estate agent. Chapter 10 looks at the skills you should possess as an agent. Chapter 11 looks at how to choose the right brokerage to join. Chapter 12 looks at how you should market yourself, your brand, and your services as an agent once you join a brokerage.

Part Four – Additional Real Estate Careers

Part four provides a more in-depth look at additional career opportunities in and related to the real estate industry. Chapter 13 looks at real estate finance. Chapter 14 looks at property management. Chapter 15 looks at real estate auctions. Chapter 16 looks at 1031 exchanges. Chapter 17 looks at residential leasing. Chapter 18 looks at commercial leasing. Finally, Chapter 19 looks at investing in real estate.

Legal Disclaimer

Although the author and publisher made every effort to ensure that the information in this book was accurate at press time, the author and publisher do not assume and hereby disclaim any liability to any party for any loss, damage, or disruption caused by errors or omissions.

The author and the publisher disclaim any and all liability to the maximum extent permitted by law if any information, analysis, opinions, advice, and/or recommendations in this book prove to be inaccurate, incomplete, unreliable, or result in any other losses.

The information contained in this book does not constitute legal or financial advice and should never be used without first consulting with legal and other professionals.

The publisher and the author do not make any guarantee or other promise as to any outcomes that may or may not be obtained from using this book's content. You should conduct your own research and due diligence.

Information in Chapters 5-9 is based on California specific real estate law and may or may not apply in your state. Laws and regulations referenced in this book are subject to change.

About the Author

David Gadish, Ph.D., is a tenured university professor, a management consultant, licensed real estate professional, real estate trainer, and coach.

David is a founding partner at Geffen Real Estate in Beverly Hills, California, where he oversees a team of residential and commercial real estate agents.

David is a professor at the College of Business and Economics, California State University, Los Angeles. He also currently teaches real estate at Touro College Los Angeles, a division of Touro University Worldwide, where he established the current real estate program.

In his spare time, David and his wife and business partner, Orit, raise their four daughters on their over 150 fruit tree orchard in Beverly Hills, California. David Gadish can be reached via text at 310-433-0694 or via email at david@GeffenRealEstate.com.

Brief Table of Contents

Motivation 4

Overview 5

Legal Disclaimer 6

About the Author 7

Brief Table of Contents 8

Table of Contents 9

Table of Figures 23

Part One – Introduction to the Real Estate Industry 25

Chapter 1 - Real Estate Basics 26

Chapter 2 – Types of Real Estate 41

Chapter 3 – Careers in the Real Estate Industry 54

Part Two – Introduction to Real Estate Sales 71

Chapter 4 - Valuation of Real Estate 72

Chapter 5 - Handling Occupied Properties 80

Chapter 6 - Handling Vacant Properties 91

Chapter 7 – Marketing Properties 106

Chapter 8 – Managing Offers 111

Chapter 9 – Managing the Escrow Process 121

Part Three – What It Takes to Succeed in Real Estate Sales 141

Chapter 10 – Skill You Should Possess 142

Chapter 11 – Choosing the Right Brokerage for You 146

Chapter 12 – Marketing Yourself, Your Brand and Your Services 155

Part Four – Additional Real Estate Careers 160

Chapter 13 – Real Estate Finance 161

Chapter 14 - Property Management 171

Chapter 15 - Real Estate Auction 177

Chapter 16 - 1031 Exchange 184

Chapter 17 - Residential Leasing 190

Chapter 18 - Commercial Leasing 202

Chapter 19 - Real Estate Investing 206

Table of Contents

Motivation 4
Overview 5
   Part One – Introduction to the Real Estate Industry 5
   Part Two – Introduction to Real Estate Sales 5
   Part Three – What It Takes to Succeed in Real Estate Sales 5
   Part Four – Additional Real Estate Careers 5
Legal Disclaimer 6
About the Author 7
Brief Table of Contents 8
Table of Contents 9
Table of Figures 23
Part One – Introduction to the Real Estate Industry 25
Chapter 1 - Real Estate Basics 26
   Chapter Overview 26
   Chapter Outline 26
   Land, Buildings, Real Estate, and Real Property 27
   The Basic Real Estate Process 27
   The Things You Can Do with Real Estate 28
      Develop Raw Land 29
      Build / Renovate 29
      Buy / Sell 29
      Lease / Rent 29
      Own for Personal Use 29
      Own for Business Use 29
      Manage 29
   Categories of Investors and/or Owners of Real Estate 30
      People 30
      Business Owners 31
      Non-Institutional Investors 31
      Institutional Investors 31
      Financial Institutions 31

- Commercial Banks 31
- Investment Banks 32
- Trust Companies 32
- Investment Brokerage Firms 32
- Insurance Companies 32
- Pension Funds 33
- Mutual Funds 33
- Real Estate Investment Trusts (REITs) 33
- Real Estate Operating Companies (REOCs) 33

Reasons to Get Involved in Real Estate 33
- Own Real Estate 34
- Make Money from Real Estate 34
- Build Real Estate 34
- Define Your Environment and That of Others 35
- Help Others 35
- To Be Creative 35

Laws and Regulations Affecting the Real Estate Industry 35
- Building Codes 36
- Zoning 36
- Entitlement 36
- Real Estate Licensing 37
- Disclosure Laws 38
- Tenant Screening 38
- Construction Licensing 38
- Antidiscrimination Laws 38
- Fair Lending Laws 38

Outlook for the Real Estate Industry 39
- Ongoing Advances in Information Technology 39
- Increased Investment in Real Estate 39
- Increased Institutional Ownership of Real Estate 39
- Increased Mergers and Acquisitions in the Real Estate Industry 40
- Increased International Investing 40

Chapter 2 – Types of Real Estate 41

- Chapter Overview 41
- Chapter Outline 41
- Types of Residential Real Estate 42
  - Single Family Detached Homes 42
  - Townhouses 42
  - Duplexes 42
  - Triplexes 43
  - Quadruplexes 43
  - Condominium Units 43
  - Mobile Homes 43
- Types of Commercial Real Estate 43
- Multi-Family (5+ Units) Properties 44
- Retail Properties 44
- Industrial Properties 45
- Office Properties 46
- Land 47
- Shopping Centers 48
- Hospitality 48
- Flex 49
- Healthcare 50
- Sports and Entertainment 51
- Specialty 51
- On Market vs. Off Market Properties (Pocket Listing) 52
- MLS, Loopnet, Costar 52
- Zoning and Property Values 53

Chapter 3 – Careers in the Real Estate Industry 54
- Chapter Overview 54
- Chapter Outline 54
- Real Estate Agent 55
  - Residential Real Estate Agent 55
  - What's the Difference: Agent, Broker, Associate Broker, Broker-Owner, Realtor? 56
  - Commercial Real Estate Agent 57
- Leasing Agent 57

Real Estate Transaction Coordinator 58
Real Estate Investor 58
Real Estate Developer 58
Real Estate Wholesaler 59
Property Manager 59
Home Inspector (Residential Inspector) 60
Commercial Inspector 60
Real Estate Appraiser 60
Real Estate Loan Officer 61
Mortgage Broker 62
Residential Mortgage Underwriter 62
Commercial Mortgage Underwriter 62
Real Estate Asset Manager 63
Foreclosure / REO Asset Manager 63
Real Estate Attorney 63
Real Estate Paralegal 64
Escrow Officer 65
Title Representative 65
Real Estate Marketing Specialist 66
Real Estate Educator / Coach 67
Licensed General Contractor 67
Licensed Landscaping Contractor 67
Professional Organizer 67
Home Stager 68
Termite and Pest Control Specialist 68
Code Compliance Retrofitting Specialist 68
Real Estate Investment Analyst 69
Real Estate Acquisitions Analyst 69
Real Estate Dispositions Analyst 69
Government / Real Estate Department Careers 69
Urban Planning Careers 70
Real Estate Research Careers 70

Part Two – Introduction to Real Estate Sales 71

Chapter 4 - Valuation of Real Estate 72
   Chapter Overview 72
   Chapter Outline 72
   Goals When Selling a Property 73
   Broker Price Opinion (BPO) 73
   Broker Price Opinion Components 73
   What is a Comparable Property? 74
   Broker Opinion of Value (BOV) 75
   Appraisal 75
   Establishing a List Price for Residential Properties 75
      First Pricing Strategy: For Ultra Luxury Properties 76
      Second Pricing Strategy: For Average Priced Properties with No Pressure to Sell Quickly 76
      Third Pricing Strategy: For Average Priced Properties with Pressure to Sell Quickly 76
   Establishing a List Price for Commercial Properties 77
      Sales Comparison Approach 78
      Cost Approach 78
      Income Capitalization Approach 78
      Gross Rent Multiplier Approach 79
      Value Per Door Approach 79

Chapter 5 - Handling Occupied Properties 80
   Chapter Overview 80
   Chapter Outline 80
   About Handling Occupied Properties 81
   Issues with Occupied Properties 81
      Legal/Illegal Units 82
      Rent Control? 82
      Unit Information 82
      No Access – No Showings? 82
      Tenant Not Paying Rent? 83
      Entering Occupied Properties with a Non-Cooperating Tenant? 83
   Relocation Assistance 83
   The Eviction Process 84
      Giving Notice 85

    The Unlawful Detainer Action 87
  Handling Abandoned Personal Property after Termination of Tenancy 88
    Landlord's Request that Tenant Retrieve Property (Residential) 89
    Delivering the Notice 89
    Format of Notice 89
    Storing Abandoned Property 89
    Releasing Abandoned Property 90
    Conducting a Public Sale of Personal Property 90
    Handling Sale Proceeds 90
    Handling Abandoned Vehicles 90

Chapter 6 - Handling Vacant Properties 91
  Chapter Overview 91
  Chapter Outline 91
  Is the Property Secure? 92
  As-Is vs. Renovate 92
    Sell As-Is 93
    Repair the Basics – Health and Safety Issues – Required by Lenders 93
    Renovate 94
    Does it "Make Sense" to Renovate? 94
  Property Preservation 94
    Rekey 95
    HOA Services and Amenities 95
    HOA FHA Approval 96
    State and Local Retrofitting Requirements 96
    Re-Inspections 96
    Organizing the Content of a Property 97
    Trashout 97
    Sales Clean 97
    Carpet Shampoo 98
    Yard Maintenance – Initial and Ongoing 98
    Pool Maintenance – Initial and Ongoing 98
    General Repairs 99
    Termite Repairs 100

- Specialized Repairs 100
- Emergency Services 100
- Hazards 101
  - Mold Damage 101
  - Fire Damage 102
  - Flood Damage 103
- Vandalism 103
  - Squatting 103
  - Dumping 104
  - Graffiti 105

Chapter 7 – Marketing Properties 106
- Chapter Overview 106
- Chapter Outline 106
- Marketing Activities 107
- Signage 107
- Professional Photos of Property 107
- Professional Video and 3D Virtual Tour 108
- Property Description 108
- Professional Website 108
- Placing the property on the MLS, LoopNet, and CoStar 109
- Traditional Marketing 109
- Online Marketing 109
- Conducting Open Houses 110
- Showing Properties 110
- Handling Price Reductions 110

Chapter 8 – Managing Offers 111
- Chapter Overview 111
- Chapter Outline 111
- The Offer Management Process 112
- Receiving Offers from Buyers / Their agents 112
- Basic Components of a Complete Offer Package 112
- State Purchase Contract/Purchase Agreement 113
- Proof of Funds (POF) 115

Loan Pre-Approval Letter (PAL) 115
Additional Components of a Complete Offer Package 115
    Gift Letter (If Applicable) 116
    Organizing Documents (if the Buyer is an Entity) 116
    Trust Documents (if the buyer is a Trust) 116
    Addenda (If Applicable) 116
Presenting Offers 117
Full Disclosure to Potential buyers 118
Selecting Offers 118
Countering Offers 119
When to Use a Counter and When to Use an Addendum 119
Assembling the Contract Package 119
Receiving, Reviewing, and Executing the Contract Package 120
Sending the Fully Executed Contract to the Buyer's Agent 120

Chapter 9 – Managing the Escrow Process 121
Chapter Overview 121
Chapter Outline 121
The Escrow Process 122
Pre-Escrow Period Activities (Phase 1): 123
    Preliminary Title Report Due Diligence 123
    Research and Handle City Pre-Sale Requirements 124
    Compile the Disclosure Package 124
    Confirm Utilities On / Turn On Utilities 125
    Order Products and Services 126
Initial Escrow Period Activities (Phase 2) 127
    Set MLS Status to Pending 127
    Send "Request to Open Escrow" Email 127
Intermediate Escrow Period Activities (Phase 3) 128
    Confirm that Escrow Received Buyer's Deposit 128
    Ensure Contingencies Are Removed 128
    Repairs During Escrow 130
    Order Home Warranty Plan 133
Activities at End of Escrow Period (Phase 4) 134

- Final Verification of Property Condition ... 134
- Contact Lender to Determine Closing Readiness ... 134
- Determine Escrow Office Readiness ... 135
- Contact Buyer's Agent to Determine Closing Readiness ... 135
- Pending to Sold Activities (Phase 5) ... 135
  - Reminder to Turn Off Utilities ... 135
  - Request Lawn/Pool Services Be Terminated ... 135
  - Remove Sign ... 135
  - Set MLS Status to Sold ... 136
- Possible Complications During the Escrow Period ... 136
  - Issue a Notice to Buyer to Perform ... 136
  - Issue Demand to Close Transaction ... 137
  - Disagreement on Release of Deposit ... 137
  - Handle Request to Change Financing Type ... 138
  - Handle Unauthorized Repairs by Buyer or Buyer's agent ... 138
  - Handle Changes in Buyers' Names on Contracts ... 138
  - Handle Vesting Change Requests ... 138
- Residential Inspections ... 138
  - General Inspection ... 138
  - Specialized Inspections ... 139
- Commercial Inspections ... 139

Part Three – What It Takes to Succeed in Real Estate Sales ... 141

Chapter 10 – Skill You Should Possess ... 142
- Chapter Overview ... 142
- Chapter Outline ... 142
- Skills Beneficial for Agents ... 143
- Ethics ... 143
- Self-Control ... 143
- Assertiveness ... 143
- Analytical Thinking ... 144
- Intuition and Creativity ... 144
- Persuasion ... 144
- Adaptability and Flexibility ... 144

Communication 144

Negotiation 145

Project Management 145

Chapter 11 – Choosing the Right Brokerage for You 146

Chapter Overview 146

Chapter Outline 146

Why is Broker Selection So Important? 147

13 Key Factors in Selecting a Real Estate Brokerage 147

Commission 148

Fees 149

Training 149

Mentoring 150

Management Support 150

Administrative Support 151

Brokerage Focus Area(s) 151

Leads and Referrals 152

Internet Presence 152

Culture 152

Brokerage Size 153

Facilities 153

Location 154

Chapter 12 – Marketing Yourself, Your Brand and Your Services 155

Chapter Overview 155

Chapter Outline 155

About Marketing Yourself, Your Brand, and Your Services 156

Your Unique Selling Proposition 156

Your Target Market Segment 156

Your Digital Footprint 157

    Website 157

    Videos 157

Your Existing Network 158

Marketing to Your Existing Network 158

Referrals from Your Existing Network 158

Expanding your Network 158

Marketing to your Expanding Network 159

Marketing Channels 159

Part Four – Additional Real Estate Careers 160

Chapter 13 – Real Estate Finance 161

Chapter Overview 161

Chapter Outline 161

About Real Estate Finance 162

Characteristics of Loans 162

    Interest Rate 162

    Amortization 162

    Repayment Period 162

    Loan to Value (LTV) 162

    Mortgage Insurance 162

    Secondary Financing 163

    Fixed vs. Adjustable-Rate Loans 163

The Four Elements to Getting a Loan 163

The Financing Process 163

    Pre-Qualification 164

    Pre-Approval 164

    Conditional Commitment Letter 164

    Formal Loan Approval 165

    Final Loan Approval 165

    Funding the Property 165

Financing Options 165

    Conventional Financing 166

    Cash, Hard Money, and Line of Credit Financing 166

    FHA Financing 167

    FHA 203K Financing 167

    VA Financing 168

    USDA Financing 168

    1031 Exchange Financing 168

    Seller Financing 169

- Private Financing 169
- Line of Credit 169
- Soft Loans 169
- Municipal Financing 170

Chapter 14 - Property Management 171
- Chapter Overview 171
- Chapter Outline 171
- About Property Management 172
- Define and Sign a Management Contract 172
- Define and Deploy Takeover Procedures 173
- Ongoing Relationship with Owner/Representative 173
- Evaluate the Property to Establish Rents 173
- Market the Property for Lease 173
- Tenant Screening, Selection, and Lease Negotiations 173
- Tenant Move-In 173
- Rent Collection 174
- Lease Renewals 174
- Tenant Relations 174
- Tenant Move Out 174
- Tenancy Termination 175
- Legal 175
- Inspections 175
- Financial Reporting 175
- Maintenance, Repair, Remodeling 175

Chapter 15 - Real Estate Auction 177
- Chapter Overview 177
- Chapter Outline 177
- About Real Estate Auctions 178
- Benefits of Real Estate Auction 178
- Differences Between Ordinary Sales and Auction Sales 179
- Auctions with Reserve 180
- Auctions Subject to Seller Confirmation 180
- Absolute Auction / Auction without Reserve 181

Important Terms of the Auction Contract 181

Bidder Registration 182

Terms Included in Auction Advertising 182

Due Diligence Prior to Auction 182

Switch to Auction if Can Not Sell via Ordinary Sale? 183

Auction Sale for Occupied Property with No Interior Access? 183

Chapter 16 - 1031 Exchange 184

Chapter Overview 184

Chapter Outline 184

About 1031 Exchanges 185

Reasons to Participate in a 1031 Exchange 185

What Can be Exchanged 185

Types of Real Estate Exchanges 185

Simultaneous 1031 Exchange 185

Delayed 1031 Exchange 186

    Sale of the Relinquished Property 186

    Identification of Replacement Property 187

    Purchase of Replacement Property 187

Reverse 1031 Exchange 187

Construction or Improvement 1031 Exchange 187

1031 Exchange Rules 188

    Exchanging Like-Kind Properties Rule 188

    Business or Investment Property Only Rule 189

    Equal or Greater Value Rule 189

    Partial 1031 Exchange Rule 189

    Exchanger Name Rule 189

    45 Day Identification Window Rule 189

    180 Day Purchase Window 189

Chapter 17 - Residential Leasing 190

Chapter Overview 190

Chapter Outline 190

About Residential Leasing 191

Defining the Terms of the Lease 191

- Commission to Agent(s) 192
- Marketing a Property for Lease 192
- Showing the Property 192
- Tenant Screening 192
  - The Lease Application 193
  - Reading a Typical Lease Application 193
  - Identifying Red Flags on Lease Applications 197
  - Common Problems with Lease Applications 198
  - Lease Application Denial Letter 198
- Lease Terms 199
- Lease Negotiations 200
- Lease Contract Management 200
- Start of Lease Term 200
- Federal and State Laws 200

Chapter 18 - Commercial Leasing 202
- Chapter Overview 202
- Chapter Outline 202
- About Commercial Leasing 203
- Components of a Commercial Leasing Application Package 203
- Application Review 203
- Types of Commercial Leases 204
- Typical Terms of Commercial Leases 204

Chapter 19 - Real Estate Investing 206
- Chapter Overview 206
- Chapter Outline 206
- About Investing in Real Estate 207
- About the Yield of Real Estate Investments 208
- About the Safety of Real Estate Investments 208
- About the Liquidity of Real Estate Investments 208
- Advantages of Investing in Real Estate 208
- Disadvantages of Investing in Real Estate 209
- Real Estate Investment Strategies 210

Table of Figures

Figure 1 - Basic Real Estate Terminology 27
Figure 2 - The Basic Real Estate Process 28
Figure 3 – The Things You Can Do with Real Estate 28
Figure 4 – Categories of Investors and/or Owners of Real Estate 30
Figure 5 – Reasons to Get Involved in Real Estate 34
Figure 6 - Real Estate Industry and Related Regulations 35
Figure 7 - Trends in Real Estate 39
Figure 8 - Types of Residential Real Estate 42
Figure 9 - Types of Commercial Real Estate 44
Figure 10 - Popular Categories of Retail Properties 45
Figure 11 - Categories of Industrial Properties 46
Figure 12 - Categories of Office Properties 47
Figure 13 - Categories of Land 47
Figure 14 - Categories of Shopping Centers 48
Figure 15 – Categories of Hospitality Properties 49
Figure 16 - Categories of Flex Properties 50
Figure 17 – Categories of Healthcare Properties 50
Figure 18 – Categories of Sports and Entertainment Properties 51
Figure 19 - Specialty Properties 51
Figure 20 - How Real Estate Professionals Introduce Themselves 56
Figure 21 - Goals for Selling Properties 73
Figure 22 - Approaches to Valuation of Commercial Real Estate 77
Figure 23 - Key Issues with Occupied Properties 81
Figure 24 – A bird's Eye View of the Eviction Process 84
Figure 25 - Renovate vs. Sell As-Is 92
Figure 26 - Property Preservation Categories 95
Figure 27 - Real Estate Marketing Activities 107
Figure 28 - Overview of the Offer Management Process 112
Figure 29 - Components of an Offer Package 113
Figure 30 - The Four Contingencies in the State Purchase Contract / Purchase Agreement 114
Figure 31 - The Escrow Process 122
Figure 32 - Possible Complications During Escrow 136
Figure 33 - Skills Agents Should Possess 143
Figure 34 – Key Factors involved in Choosing the Right Brokerage for you 148
Figure 35 - Four Elements to Getting Financing 163
Figure 36 - The Financing Process 164
Figure 37 - Types of Real Estate Financing 166
Figure 38 - Key Property Management Activities 172
Figure 39 - Benefits of Real Estate Auction 179
Figure 40 - Delayed Exchange Timeline 186

Figure 41 - 1031 Exchange Rules 188
Figure 42 - The Residential Leasing Process 191
Figure 43 - Lease Application Components 194
Figure 44 - Typical Residential Lease Terms 199
Figure 45 - Types of Real Estate Returns 207
Figure 46 - Key Investment Characteristics 207
Figure 47 - Advantages of Investing in Real Estate 209
Figure 48 - Disadvantages of Investing in Real Estate 209

Part One – Introduction to the Real Estate Industry

Part one of the book provides an overview of real estate and real estate careers. Chapter 1 introduces the basics of real estate as well as of the real estate industry. Chapter 2 looks at the different types of residential as well as commercial real estate. Chapter 3 provides a survey of 35 real estate and related careers.

Chapter 1 - Real Estate Basics

Chapter Overview

Chapter 1 provides an introduction to real estate and the real estate industry. It looks at some basic definitions and aims to answer a few basic questions about real estate. The chapter proceeds to survey key regulations of the industry and significant trends in it.

If you are familiar with these basics, you can scan through this chapter and then proceed to the next one.

Chapter Outline

Land, Buildings, Real Estate, and Real Property

The Basic Real Estate Process

What Can You Do with Real Estate?

Who Invests in Real Estate?

Why Get Involved in Real Estate?

Laws and Regulations Affecting the Real Estate Industry

Trends in Real Estate

Land, Buildings, Real Estate, and Real Property

Basic terminology repeatedly used throughout this book includes (see Figure 1):

- **Land** is often defined as the earth's surface as well as what is below and above the surface, including the trees, water, and minerals.
- **Buildings** are often defined as roofed and walled structures built for permanent use.
- **Real Estate** is often defined as the land, plus any buildings on it. The buildings may be residential or commercial. It may also include in-ground pools, walkways leading to detached garages, and the garages themselves located on the property.
- **Real Property** is often defined as real estate and the interests, benefits, and rights inherent in its ownership.

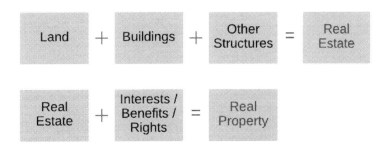

Figure 1 - Basic Real Estate Terminology

Often, people speak of or write about real estate when they are referring to real property. For this reason, this book takes the same approach.

The Basic Real Estate Process

Developers acquire land and develop it into residential or commercial real estate assets by constructing buildings and other structures on the land. Some developers hold on to the assets they develop and lease them to tenants (residential or commercial). Other developers sell their assets to investors or owner-occupants. Investors who purchase assets from developers either hold on to them and lease them out to tenants or sell them to owner-occupants (see Figure 2).

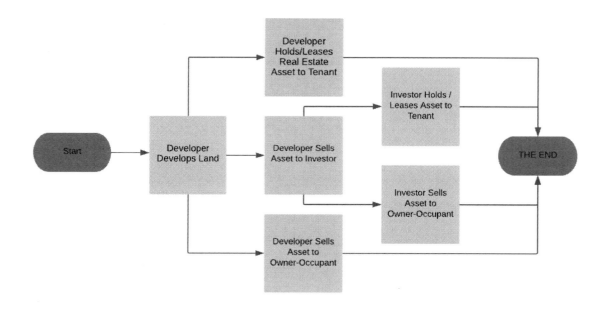

Figure 2 - The Basic Real Estate Process

The Things You Can Do with Real Estate

So much can be done with real estate (see Figure 3). You can develop raw land, build new buildings, or renovate existing ones. You can buy, sell, rent/lease real estate. You can use real estate for your own personal or professional/business use. And, you can manage real estate for others.

Figure 3 – The Things You Can Do with Real Estate

Develop Raw Land
You can develop raw land into real estate by building structures on the land. You need to follow local building codes and zoning regulations (discussed later in the book).

Build / Renovate
You can tear down existing commercial or residential buildings and build new ones. You can add square footage to existing buildings. You can renovate buildings with or without adding square footage. You can renovate for yourself to live and/or work in, generate income, or both.

Buy / Sell
You can buy and sell real estate for yourself or help others purchase and/or sell real estate. You do not need a real estate license to buy and sell real estate for yourself, but you need a license if you plan to help others (in most states).

Purchasing real estate is also known as real estate **Acquisition**. Selling real estate is also known as real estate **Disposition**.

Lease / Rent
A **Rental** is short term tenancy (usually 30 days) that is automatically renewed unless either party gives notice. A **Lease** is typically for 12 months but can be much longer as well. When a lease expires, it does not usually automatically renew itself.

You do not need a real estate license to lease real estate for your own use from others or lease your real estate to others, but you do need a license if you plan to help others with their leasing needs (in most states).

Own for Personal Use
You can own real estate for your personal use. You can own a single-family residence or a condo. Some people own vacation homes. Others own duplexes, triplexes, or quads and live in one of the units while collecting income on the others.

Own for Business Use
You can use real estate to operate your business from. You can own your office building, retail store, warehouse, or any other type of commercial real estate (discussed in Chapter 2) and operate your business(es) from them.

Manage
You can manage your own real estate assets, and/or you can help manage real estate belonging to others.

You do not need a real estate license to manage your own real estate, but you do need a license if you plan to help others manage theirs (in most states).

Categories of Investors and/or Owners of Real Estate

Almost anyone can own real estate! (see Figure 4). People, non-institutional investors, business owners can all own real estate. Other real estate owners include financial institutions, commercial banks, investment banks, trust companies, investment brokerage firms, insurance companies, pension funds, mutual funds, real estate investment trusts, and real estate operating companies.

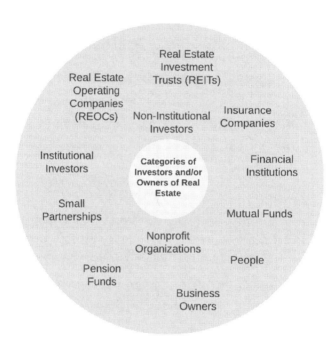

Figure 4 – Categories of Investors and/or Owners of Real Estate

People

About 64 percent of US households own their homes, and about 36 percent rent their homes.

You can find properties with buildings on them for as little as a few thousand dollars in certain parts of the country. You can also get close to 100 percent financing on some properties and depending on your financial situation.

Most people purchase residential real estate put down 3% to 20%, and finance the rest.

Business Owners

While most business owners lease the space from which they operate, hundreds of thousands of business owners throughout the country own the real estate from which they run their businesses.

Non-Institutional Investors

Real estate investors can be one or more individuals that purchase real estate, and then:

- Lease the properties in their as-is condition
- Fix and flip the properties
- Fix and lease the properties

Some are focused on the short-term while others on long-term returns on their investments.

Institutional Investors

Institutional investors are companies that invest money on behalf of other people. Examples include banks, mutual funds, pension funds, and insurance companies. Institutional investors frequently buy and sell substantial blocks of bonds, stocks, and other securities.

Financial Institutions

Financial Institutions are organizations focused on financial and monetary transactions such as deposits, loans, and investments. Financial institutions offer different products and services for individuals and business clients. Financial institutions include commercial banks, investment banks, trust companies, brokerage firms, and insurance companies. An overview of each type of institution is provided next.

Commercial Banks

A commercial bank is a type of financial institution that provides the following services to individuals and businesses:

- Deposit services
- Checking account services
- Personal loans
- Business loans
- Home mortgages
- Certificates of deposit (CDs) and savings accounts for individuals and businesses.
- Credit card services
- Wire transfer services
- Currency exchange services

Many commercial banks also typically provide home mortgages. Some are also focused on providing commercial real estate loans.

Investment Banks

Investment banks provide services that facilitate:

- Capital expenditure financing for businesses
- Equity offerings (e.g., selling stock in a corporation, including Initial public offerings - IPOs).
- Brokerage services for investors
- Mergers, acquisitions, and other corporate restructurings

Investment banks also provide real estate specific services, including:

- Issuing Mortgage-Backed Securities (MBS) on residential as well as commercial properties
- Originating stocks and bonds for real estate companies.
- Investing in residential and/or commercial real estate directly
- Investing in residential and/or commercial real estate through funds
- Selling REIT stocks

Trust Companies

Trust companies are legal entities that act as fiduciaries, agents, or trustees on behalf of persons or businesses. They administer, manage and eventually transfer assets, including real estate assets, to the beneficiaries.

Investment Brokerage Firms

Brokerage firms provide investment services that include:

- Wealth management services
- Financial advisory services
- Access to investment products (stocks, bonds, hedge funds, and private equity investments)

Investment brokerages provide investment services in various asset classes, including residential and commercial real estate.

Insurance Companies

Insurance companies provide insurance to individuals and/or corporations. They provide asset protection as well as protection against financial risk.

The premiums that they collect from insurance policies are invested in various investment classes. A significant portion of these investments is directed into real estate. Teams of analysts look at different real estate investment vehicles, and then teams of investment managers handle the actual investing. The amount invested in real estate has been growing yearly in recent years.

Pension Funds
Pension funds invest billions of dollars of employee and employer pension funds in various investment classes. A significant portion of these investments is directed into real estate. Teams of analysts look at different real estate investment vehicles, and then teams of investment managers handle the actual investing. The amount invested in real estate has been growing yearly in recent years.

Mutual Funds
Mutual funds pool money from investors and use that money to buy securities, such as stocks and bonds. Real estate mutual funds typically invest in real estate related stocks, REIT stocks, or both.

Real Estate Investment Trusts (REITs)
Real Estate Investment Trusts (REITs) are companies that invest and own real estate properties or mortgages. They also often operate the real estate they own. There are three types of REITs.

- Equity REITs own and invest in commercial and/or residential properties. Revenues are generated mainly from the rents.
- Mortgage REITs invest in residential and commercial mortgages—these REITs loan money for mortgages or purchase existing mortgages or mortgage-backed securities (MBS). Revenues are generated primarily from interest earned on the mortgages.
- Hybrid REITs invest in properties as well as in mortgages.

The Internal Revenue Service (IRS) requires REITs to pay out most of their taxable profits to shareholders via dividends.

Real Estate Operating Companies (REOCs)
Real Estate Operating Companies (REOCs) are companies that engage in real estate investments and whose shares are traded on a public exchange.

They can buy and sell real estate. They can also develop, manage, and own real estate. REOCs can re-invest the money they earn back into their business, but they are subject to standard corporate taxes (higher corporate taxes than REITs).

Reasons to Get Involved in Real Estate
There are many reasons to get involved in real estate (see Figure 5). People get involved in real estate to own it, make money from it, build it, shape the environment, help others, and be creative.

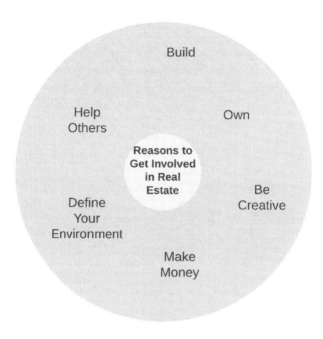

Figure 5 – Reasons to Get Involved in Real Estate

Let us look at these reasons to get involved in real estate in more detail.

Own Real Estate

If you would like to own real estate assets beyond your primary residence, consider getting involved in real estate.

The more you know about real estate, the more likely you will uncover better acquisition opportunities for yourself.

Make Money from Real Estate

If you are thinking about making big money, real estate might be the way to get there. Purchasing real estate is, for most people, their largest expenditure, and a sizable commission follows.

You can generate substantial income in any business if you are great at marketing, sales, and delivering quality products or services, followed by excellent customer service. Many businesses have high barriers to entry. A high barrier to entry is not the case with real estate sales.

Build Real Estate

If you like to see homes built, like to build homes, or would like to build homes, consider learning more about residential real estate.

If you like to see certain types of commercial buildings built, like to build them, or would like to build them, consider learning more about commercial real estate.

Define Your Environment and That of Others
If you want to define the environment and the way neighborhoods, and cities look, real estate might be for you.

Help Others
And, of course, real estate is all about helping others. You can help people buy, sell, lease, finance, manage, or build real estate.

There are 10s of career paths in and related to real estate, and they are explored in Chapter 3.

To Be Creative
If you like to be creative and work in an environment where each day is different, consider getting involved in real estate.

Dealing with vast amounts of money and/or amplified human emotions guarantees endless surprises, which could benefit from your creativity.

Laws and Regulations Affecting the Real Estate Industry
There are different categories of laws and regulations that affect the real estate industry (see Figure 6)

Figure 6 - Real Estate Industry and Related Regulations

The following is a brief look at these key categories of laws and regulations related to the real estate industry.

Building Codes

These are regulations adopted by local governments to govern the use of land and construction of buildings and other structures on it. Building codes are intended to protect buildings and the people and property inside them from:

- Floods
- Fire
- Earthquakes
- Other extreme events

Their goal is to maximize:

- Structural integrity
- Electrical system safety
- Plumbing system safety
- Mechanical system safety
- Energy efficiency

Zoning

Zoning is a process and the laws defined by local municipalities that divide land into zones for different uses. Land is usually split into zones for residential, industrial, or commercial use. Typically there are various residential zones, various industrial zones, and various commercial zones. Each zone has specific limitations on the size, density, and location of buildings and other structures.

If land is not zoned for the use you want, you will have to apply for rezoning. In some cases, where you need certain adjustments made, you can request a zoning variance.

Entitlement

While zoning codes predetermine what certain land can be used for, entitlement is an approval that must be gained from the government to develop land the way you want, when you want to build something on land, but the current zoning does not allow it.

The entitlement process is typically lengthy and complicated, and before granting entitlement, governments will consider various variables, including traffic impacts, environmental risk, and community responses to potential development.

Without going through the process, your structure might be subject to modifications, fines, and possible demolition.

Types of entitlements:

- **Rezoning**: A property's zoning indicates what you can and can not do with the land. If the area is not zoned for your planned use, you may need to go through the rezoning process. Rezoning can be complicated and lengthy. Sometimes, it is not allowed or not possible.
- **Zoning variances**: This can include items such as building heights and setbacks.
- **Use permits:** Conditional use permit for your project.
- **Utility approvals**: Approval for utilities that are not currently at the site.
- **Road approvals**: Approval for paving road(s) to connect to your property.

Real Estate Licensing

The purpose is to help regulate the real estate profession and protect the public. Typically, a real estate license is required by anyone acting as a real estate salesperson/broker (acting on behalf of someone else for compensation or expected compensation).

Different states have different requirements. Use an online search engine to search "real estate license requirements for <your state>" to find those for your state. As an example, in California, see: https://www.dre.ca.gov/examinees/RequirementsSales.html

In California, the successful completion of three college-level courses is required to qualify for a real estate salesperson examination:

- Real Estate Principles
- Real Estate Practice
- One course from the following list:
    - Real Estate Appraisal
    - Property Management
    - Real Estate Finance
    - Real Estate Economics
    - Legal Aspects of Real Estate
    - Real Estate Office Administration
    - General Accounting
    - Business Law
    - Escrows
    - Mortgage Loan Brokering and Lending
    - Computer Applications in Real Estate
    - Common Interest Developments

Courses must be three semester-units or four quarter-units at the college level. Courses must be completed at an institution of higher learning accredited by the Western Association of Schools and Colleges or by a comparable regional accrediting agency recognized by the United States Department of Education or by a private real estate school with its courses approved by the California Real Estate Commissioner. Each course approved by the Department of Real Estate is a minimum of 45 hours in length.

Disclosure Laws

Latent defects are issues not discoverable by ordinary inspection. If a licensed real estate agent is aware of any such defects, they must disclose them in writing to other parties to a transaction.

Lead-based paint involves properties built before 1978. The paint poses a health risk, and its existence must be disclosed to potential buyers and tenants.

Megan's law requires the disclosure of known registered sex offenders living in a property's vicinity to potential buyers and tenants.

Tenant Screening

The Fair Credit Reporting Act requires that if you use a credit report to reject a candidate tenant, you should inform them of this in writing.

The USA PATRIOT Act requires property managers not to enter into contracts with candidate tenants listed on the Specially Designated Nationals and Blocked Persons List. They should also be reported to the Office of Foreign Assets Control of the federal government.

Construction Licensing

Many states require the licensing of contractors. Using a licensed contractor can reduce your financial risk, legal risk, and other problems associated with unlicensed individuals performing construction work.

In California, for example, anyone who contracts to perform work on a project that is valued at $500 or more for combined labor and materials costs must hold a current, valid license from the Contractors State License Board.

Antidiscrimination Laws

Various laws, including the Civil Rights Acts, the Fair Housing Act, and Americans with Disabilities Act combined make it illegal to discriminate based on race, color, religion, sex, sexual orientation, gender identity, age, ethnicity, national origin, disability, or family status in the sale or lease of residential real estate.

For example, Steering is prohibited. This means that real estate agents are not allowed to limits the housing options available to a buyer or tenants by directing them to different neighborhoods or communities or even different parts of the same development based on their race or other characteristics protected under the Fair Housing Act.

Fair Lending Laws

The federal fair lending laws, the Equal Credit Opportunity Act and the Fair Housing Act, prohibit discrimination by lenders in credit transactions, including transactions related to residential real estate.

Outlook for the Real Estate Industry

The real estate industry is continuing to shift. More advances in automating are likely to affect all involved in the industry. Industry consolidations, increased institutional ownership, increased global investing, and increased investments in real estate are all likely to continue (see Figure 7).

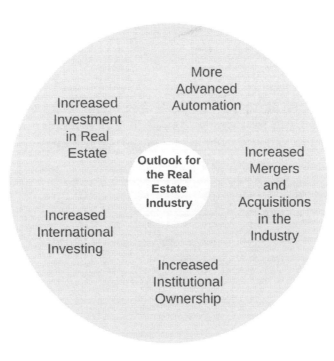

Figure 7 - Trends in Real Estate

Ongoing Advances in Information Technology

More and more companies invest millions of dollars in automating more and more real estate processes, eliminating more and more traditional real estate jobs in the process. While this trend is not specific to the real estate industry, its impact each year is immense, with no end in sight.

Increased Investment in Real Estate

More and more capital has been invested in real estate in recent years. More and more capital has become available for the development of real estate projects. More and more companies need employees with real estate related education and/or experience.

Increased Institutional Ownership of Real Estate

More and more large institutional players are investing in real estate, and more and more smaller investors get pushed aside. These large players include REITS, REOCs, insurance companies, pension funds, and others. These institutional players need more and more employees with real estate education and background to join their ranks.

Increased Mergers and Acquisitions in the Real Estate Industry
More and more large players with deep pockets have moved into the real estate industry in recent decades. They are merging with one another and acquiring others. There are still many small companies in real estate and a selection of large ones. Larger companies may own portfolios of billions of dollars worth of real estate and offer a wider variety of real estate jobs.

Increased International Investing
US companies are developing and investing in real estate all over the world. And Non-US companies are inversing in real estate opportunities throughout the US. Getting involved with such companies may provide you with travel and/or work abroad opportunities.

Chapter 2 – Types of Real Estate

Chapter Overview

Chapter 2 provides a survey of the different types of residential and commercial real estate and their characteristics. It proceeds to discuss the distinction between listing properties on and off-market. It concludes with a discussion of online services where such listings are placed on the market.

Some real estate professionals handle various types of real estate, while others choose to specialize in one or more types.

Chapter Outline

Types of Residential Real Estate

Types of Commercial Real Estate

On Market vs. Off Market Properties (Pocket Listing)

MLS, Loopnet, Costar

Types of Residential Real Estate

Types of residential real estate include single-family, townhomes, duplexes, triplexes, quadruplexes, and condominium units (See Figure 8). Residential real estate can be owner-occupied, serve as an income property, or be a combination of the two.

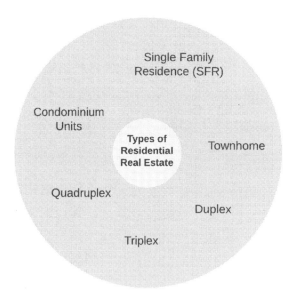

Figure 8 - Types of Residential Real Estate

Single Family Detached Homes

Various people and organizations define single-family homes slightly differently. Typically, the building has direct access to the street, one kitchen, and heating, water, and other services are not shared with any other unit.

Townhouses

Townhouses are defined as single-family dwellings with at least two floors that share a wall with another house. Unlike duplexes, triplexes, or fourplexes, however, each townhouse is individually owned.

Duplexes

Duplexes are single buildings with two living units in them. The two units could be side by side or on top of each other. Each unit must have a separate entrance, kitchen, bathroom, and utility meters. Each unit has the same features you would see in a typical single-family detached home.

Triplexes

Triplexes are single buildings with three living units in them. The three units could be side by side, one on top of the other or a combination of the two. Each unit must have a separate entrance, kitchen, bathroom, and utility meters. Each unit has the same amenities you would see in a typical single-family detached home.

Quadruplexes

Quadruplexes are single buildings with four living units in them. The four units could be side by side, one on top of the other, or a combination of. Each unit must have a separate entrance, kitchen, bathroom, and utility meters. Each unit has the same amenities you would see in a typical single-family detached home.

Condominium Units

A condominium is a property complex divided into individual units and sold to different parties. Condominium unit ownership usually includes a nonexclusive interest in community property handled by the condominium management. Condominium management is usually made up of a board. The board comprises condominium unit owners who oversee the complex's operation, such as building security and lawn maintenance.

Condo owners own the air space inside their condo units and share an ownership interest in the community property, such as the land, floor, walls, sidewalks, stairwells, and exterior areas.

Condo owners make monthly payments to a Homeowner's Association (HOA), which is in charge of property upkeep.

The key difference between an apartment and a condo unit is ownership. An apartment is a unit rented from the owner of the whole building, while an individual owner owns a condo.

Mobile Homes

A mobile home is a transportable prefabricated structure built on a steel chassis situated in one place, connected to utilities, and used as permanent living accommodation.

In California, for example, real estate agents can sell used manufactured homes and mobile homes that have previously been sold or placed on a foundation system. Please check online the situation in your state.

Types of Commercial Real Estate

Types of commercial real estate include multi-family (5+ units), retail, industrial, office, land, shopping centers, hospitality, flex, healthcare, sports and entertainment, student housing, and others (see Figure 9).

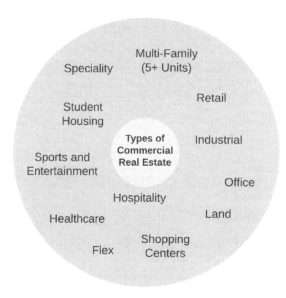

Figure 9 - Types of Commercial Real Estate

Multi-Family (5+ Units) Properties

Multi-Family Properties of five or more units are considered to be commercial properties. Some laws, such as RESPA, do not apply to 5+ unit properties.

Multi-Family properties are often classified as low rise, mid-rise, high-rise, or garden style.

Some states, counties, and/or cities have rent control ordinances, which means that buildings built before a specific date are subject to limited annual rent increases as well as additional rules that favor tenants.

Investors typically look at properties in a range of units. So some may be interested in 5-12 units, others only in 8 units, etc. They are also interested in the unit mix (# of Studios, # of 1Bed/1Bath, etc.). They look at the physical condition (Excellent /Good / Deferred Maintenance), percent occupancy, the price per unit (per door), and of course, parking and location.

Retail Properties

Retail properties are used to market and sell consumer goods and services. They include (see Figure 10): auto dealerships, auto repair shops, banks, bars, bowling alleys, convenience stores, daycare centers, department stores, drug stores, fast food, funeral homes, garden centers, health club, movie theatres, restaurants, retail buildings, service stations, storefronts, supermarkets, truck stops, and veterinarians/kennels.

Investors of retail properties typically look at a specific range of square footage of interest to them. Some investors like single-tenant retail, others like multi-tenant retail.

Investors also look at the location, proximity to other business establishments, property condition, type, and quality of existing tenants. Some investors like vacant retail.

Figure 10 - Popular Categories of Retail Properties

Industrial Properties

Industrial properties accommodate industrial activities, including production, manufacturing, assembly, warehousing, research, storage, and distribution.

Industrial properties include (see Figure 11): distribution centers, food processing facilities, manufacturing, refrigeration/cold storage, service warehouses, showrooms, data/hosting centers, truck terminals, and warehouses.

Investors or owner-occupants looking for industrial properties focus on location, proximity to freeways and railroads, specific ranges of square footage, number of tenants, age, loading docks, ceiling height, lot size, parking, type of construction.

Figure 11 - Categories of Industrial Properties

Office Properties

An office is generally a building or a portion of a building where an organization's employees perform administrative work in support of its goals.

Office properties include (see Figure 12): live/work units, lofts/creative spaces, medical office spaces, and of course, office buildings.

Investors or owner-occupants looking for office properties focus on square footage, class (A/B/C/D), range of stories, tenancy (single/multiple), physical condition, percent occupancy, location, parking ratio, parking type, building features, construction type, number of elevators and more.

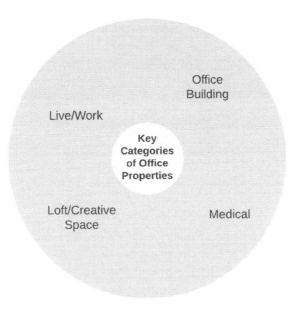

Figure 12 - Categories of Office Properties

Land

Land is often defined as the earth's surface down to the center of the earth and up to the airspace above, including the trees, water, and minerals.

Vacant land is typically zoned for residential, commercial, industrial, or agricultural uses (see Figure 13).

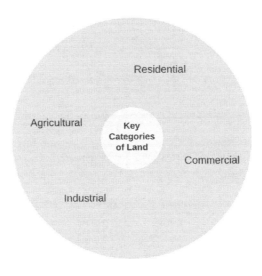

Figure 13 - Categories of Land

Shopping Centers

A Shopping Center is a group of stores (retailers/merchants) and/or service providers typically with on-site parking and storefront identity signage. The size and configuration are dependent on the purpose and the Trade Area that they serve. A **Trade Area** is the geographic area from which a shopping center attains its customers.

Categories of shopping centers include (see Figure 14): airport retail, neighborhood centers, regional centers, super-regional centers, community shopping centers, outlet malls, theme/festival centers, lifestyle centers, power centers, and strip shopping centers.

Investors looking for shopping centers focus on specific ranges of square footage, the number of tenants, location, traffic count, property condition, CAP rate, parking type and parking spaces, anchor tenants, and tenant mix and length of leases.

Figure 14 - Categories of Shopping Centers

Hospitality

Hospitality property categories include (see Figure 15) all types of lodging facilities, including hotels, motels, and casinos.

Hotels offer lodging accommodations and a wide range of other services such as restaurants, casinos, convention facilities, meeting rooms, recreational facilities, and commercial shops. Hotels can be labeled Resort, Mixed Use, Luxury, Full Service, Extended Stay, Convention, Apartment, All-Suite, and more.

Motels are single buildings or groups of buildings typically located near freeways and serve travelers' needs by offering lodging and parking. They may also provide food and beverages, meeting and banquet rooms, a swimming pool and/or a shop.

Single Room Occupancy (SRO) Hotels cater to very low-income individuals. They provide small rooms with a bed, chair, possibly a small desk and a small fridge. Occupants share the toilets, bathrooms, and kitchen.

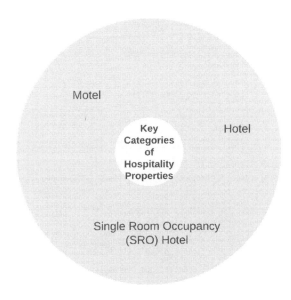

Figure 15 – Categories of Hospitality Properties

Flex

Flex buildings are designed to be multi-purpose. They can be used for any of: office (corporate headquarters), research and development, quasi-retail sales with any of: industrial, warehouse, and distribution uses. At least 50 percent of the rentable area of the building must be used as office space.

Key categories of flex properties include (see Figure 16): light distribution, light manufacturing, Research and Development (R&D), showrooms.

Figure 16 - Categories of Flex Properties

Healthcare

The healthcare properties category includes (see Figure 17): assisted living facilities, congregate senior housing, continuing care retirement communities, hospitals, rehabilitation centers, and skilled nursing facilities.

Investors looking for healthcare properties focus on specific categories of healthcare facilities. Some want to purchase the license to operate the facility and the real estate; others concentrate on purchasing the real estate. They also look at age, the number of rooms, beds per room, location, physical condition, square footage, parking, and percent occupancy.

Figure 17 – Categories of Healthcare Properties

Sports and Entertainment

The sports and Entertainment properties category includes (see Figure 18): swimming pools, sports fields, theatres/concert halls, golf courses, horse stables, amusement parks, race tracks, and skating rinks.

Figure 18 – Categories of Sports and Entertainment Properties

Specialty

The specialty category includes commercial properties that are not in any of the categories discussed in previous sections (see Figure 19). Specialty properties include (but are not limited to): airports, auto salvage facilities, car washes, cement plants, cemeteries, refineries, correctional facilities, landfill sites, lodge/meeting halls, lumberyards, marinas, movie /TV studios, parking garages, parking lots, Public Libraries, recycling centers, religious facilities, schools, self-storage facilities, student housing, trailer/camper parks, and vineyards.

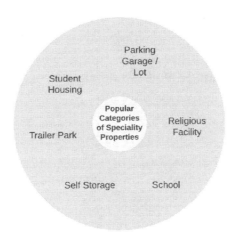

Figure 19 - Specialty Properties

On Market vs. Off Market Properties (Pocket Listing)

Most residential properties are bought or sold "On Market". This means to market a property for sale; real estate agents enter information about the property offered for sale on the appropriate Multiple Listing Service (MLS), an online portal for marketing properties associated with the local association of Realtors.

Once a property is entered into an MLS system, it is almost immediately propagated to www.Realtor.com, www.Zillow.com, www.Redfin.com, and 100+ other websites. This is handled automatically by the MLS and does not require additional effort. A "yes/no" field typically allows the agent to propagate or not propagate to various sites on the internet.

However, some residential properties are sold "Off Market", which means they are not entered into the MLS system and therefore are not propagated to other websites. While there are several valid reasons for selling off-market, it is usually not the best approach, as discussed later in the book.

Commercial properties are sold both on and off-market. Agents typically encourage commercial owners to sell off-market; this way, they can shop the deal around and double-end the deal (get paid for representing both sides). While this is great for the agent, this does not benefit the seller since it does not maximize commercial property's exposure. Also, representing both buyer and seller poses risks and may lead to legal matters due to lack of fiduciary duty to one of the parties.

However, many commercial owners are concerned that placing their property on the market could reduce the purchase price. The reasoning here is that some existing tenants might get scared, thinking the new owner would increase their rents, and start looking to move. Reduced income from tenants equates to lower sales prices.

MLS, Loopnet, Costar

The local MLS is where agents list their residential properties for sale. In addition to numerous property details, agents provide:

- **Public Remarks** - showcase the features of the property
- **Private Remarks** - are seen by agents only and include specific instructions that listing agents provide to buyers' agents interested in the property
- **Showing instructions** - indicate what needs to be done to see the property

Your local MLS might allow you to list commercial assets, and some agents list commercial assets for sale on their local MLS. Most commercial assets should, however, also be listed on Loopnet.com and CoStar.com. These are online marketplaces for commercial properties for sale and lease throughout the United States.

Investors and reputable commercial agents all know to go to these online platforms when looking to purchase commercial assets for their clients.

Zoning and Property Values

The zoning of a property affects its value. You can always double-check the zoning of the property you are handling by looking at the title profile available through your local MLS or your local title representative. To understand the zoning's significance, search online the name of your city and the term "zoning regulations".

Over time, you will learn the meaning and the financial significance of having a property in different zones. For example, a Single Family Residence (SFR) on an R-1 zone in Los Angeles is worth substantially less than a similar SFR on an R-3 or R-4 zoned lot nearby. This is the case since one could tear down the existing structure and build a multi-family apartment or condo building on an R-4 or R-3 lot but not on an R-1 zoned lot.

Also, consider two lots of identical size across the street from each other. One lot is an R-3 and the other an R-4. The R-4 lot could sell for substantially more than the R-3 lot since it is possible to build an apartment building with many more units on an R-4 than an R-3 lot. You will learn to identify these and many other scenarios related to zoning and market the properties accordingly to maximize their returns.

Chapter 3 – Careers in the Real Estate Industry

Chapter Overview

Chapter 3 provides a survey of the wide range of careers in and surrounding the real estate industry.

This chapter looks at real estate sales, leasing, development, wholesale, and property management. It then proceeds to look at other related careers.

Chapter Outline

- Real Estate Agent
- Residential Real Estate Agent
- What's the Difference: Agent, Broker, Associate Broker, Broker-Owner, Realtor?
- Commercial Real Estate Agent
- Leasing Agent
- Real Estate Investor
- Real Estate Developer
- Real Estate Wholesaler
- Property Manager
- Home Inspector (Residential Inspector)
- Commercial Inspector
- Real Estate Appraiser
- Real Estate Loan Officer
- Mortgage Broker
- Mortgage Underwriter
- Real Estate Asset Manager
- Foreclosure / REO Asset Manager
- Real Estate Attorney
- Escrow Officer
- Title Representative
- Real Estate Marketing Specialist
- Real Estate Educator / Coach
- Licensed General Contractor
- Licensed Landscaping Contractor
- Professional Organizer
- Home Stager
- Termite and Pest Control Specialist
- Code Compliance Retrofitting Specialist
- Government / Real Estate Department Careers
- Urban Planning Careers
- Real Estate Research Careers

Real Estate Agent

A Real Estate Agent career is the most common real estate career people pursue. Real estate agents help people sell or buy properties. You can be a buyers' agent representing buyers or a listing agent representing sellers, or both. You can also be either a residential agent, a commercial agent, or both. You will need a real estate license to practice as a real estate agent in most states.

Residential Real Estate Agent

Residential real estate agents facilitate the home buying process between sellers and buyers. To be successful, you need an effective lead generation and conversion strategy. Real estate is mostly marketing, so you need to enjoy doing that. You also need to provide excellent service to your clients. Excellent service results in positive reviews online, client referrals, and repeat business.

It is essential to join a brokerage where you can be mentored by the broker or another person assigned to mentor you.

You can also typically take various courses at your local association of realtors and become certified in any of several specialties.

Some agents handle all residential properties, while others specialize in one or more specific property types:

- Single-family homes
- Condominiums (Condos)
- Luxury homes
- Vacation homes
- Foreclosures/REOs
- Probate properties

Your state association of realtors may offer a variety of certifications, such as:

- First-time buyer specialist
- Investment property specialist
- Probate and trust specialist
- Buyer's representative
- International property specialist
- Military relocation professional
- Resort and second home specialist
- Senior real estate specialist
- Short sale and foreclosure specialist

Some agents focus on representing sellers; some focus on representing buyers, others focus on both. Representing sellers typically requires developing deep relations with people until years later, your growing reputation starts to bring sellers knocking on your door. In this role, you will price properties, market properties, review offers, negotiate with buyers' agents, and manage the escrow process to close.

Representing buyers involves deep relations as well. In this role, you will present buyers with properties that match their criteria, show those properties they are interested in, help determine what price and terms to offer for the property they would like to purchase, write offers, negotiate terms, and manage the escrow process to close.

For more information about this career path, you can visit:

- National Association of Realtors - www.nar.realtor
- Check online for your specific state and local associations. For example, in California: California Association of Realtors - www.car.org – example of a state-level organization of realtors, and Greater Los Angeles Realtors - www.bhglaar.com – example of a local association of Realtors

What's the Difference: Agent, Broker, Associate Broker, Broker-Owner, Realtor?

Real estate professionals introduce themselves in different ways. Figure 20 below shows how real estate professionals introduce themselves in California. Check online how this differs in your state.

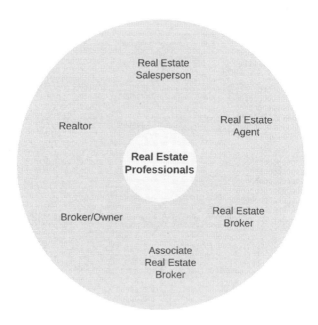

Figure 20 - How Real Estate Professionals Introduce Themselves

The following are some definitions:

- **Real Estate Salesperson** – To qualify to become a salesperson, an individual must complete three courses and apply and pass the California Department of Real Estate's state exam. A Salesperson must work under a Broker's supervision. The standard is not very high, and there are nearly 300,000 licensed individuals in

California, according to the California Department of Real Estate (2020), and over 2 million throughout the US.
- **Real Estate Agent** – Same as Real Estate Salesperson
- **Real Estate Broker** – Typically requires two years of full-time working experience as a real estate agent, completing eight courses, and passing a state exam. A broker can work independently by establishing a brokerage. They can also work under the supervision of another broker, in which case the broker is referred to as an "Associate Broker". There are 131,000 brokers, according to the California Department of Real Estate (2020).
- **Associate Real Estate Broker** - A person with a Broker's license and is working under another broker's supervision.
- **Broker-Owner** – An individual who has his/her own brokerage and may have a team of one or more real estate agents and/or brokers (associate brokers) working under the Broker-Owner's supervision.
- **Realtor** – An agent or broker that is also a member of the National Association of Realtors (NAR). Realtors are required to follow the NAR Code of Ethics.

This book will refer to an individual practicing real estate as a real estate agent, or simply an "agent".

Commercial Real Estate Agent

Commercial real estate agents handle commercial real estate assets (those discussed earlier in Chapter 2). As in residential real estate, marketing and excellent service are essential. Commercial agents work with data like capitalization rates (CAP), gross rent multipliers (GRM), and internal rates of return (IRR). Therefore, you need to like to work with numbers to perform analysis, and having some business and financial knowledge is also beneficial.

Commercial real estate agents help businesses find locations that fit their needs. They help individuals and companies that wish to invest in commercial real estate assets identify, negotiate, and purchase such assets. Some agents focus on leasing, others on sales.

Commercial agents often must uncover statistics and data about the area before they commence a transaction.

For more information about this career path, you can visit:

- Certified Commercial Investment Member Institute - www.CCIM.com
- The Society of Industrial and Office Realtors - www.sior.com

Leasing Agent

Leasing agents work with property owners/landlords to find suitable tenants to lease their rental properties too. Other leasing agents work with tenants or both owners and tenants. You can focus on residential leasing, commercial leasing, or both. If you choose to deal with commercial properties, you can further specialize in a specific commercial property type.

You will need a real estate license to practice as a leasing agent. To be successful, you need an effective lead generation and conversion strategy. Real estate is mostly marketing, so you need to enjoy doing that. You need to provide top service to your clients. You also need excellent communication and negotiation skills to be successful at real estate leasing. Residential leasing is covered in Chapter 17, and commercial leasing in Chapter 18.

For more information about this career path, you can visit:

- National Association of Realtors - www.nar.realtor
- Check online for your specific state and local associations. For example, in California: California Association of Realtors - www.car.org – example of a state-level organization of realtors, and Greater Los Angeles Realtors - www.bhglaar.com – example of a local association of Realtors

Real Estate Transaction Coordinator

Transaction coordinators help real estate agents write offers and oversee the escrow process from start to finish. Some transaction coordinators interface with the agent's clients while others do not, depending on the agent's operational strategy. If you are not excited about dealing directly with buyers and sellers and are detail-oriented, this career path may be worth exploring further.

For more information about this career path, you can visit:

- National Association of Real Estate Support Professionals - www.naresp.org

Real Estate Investor

There are two types of real estate investors: active investors and passive investors.

Active real estate investors buy residential and/or commercial real estate. They may buy-and-hold as is, buy-add value-and-hold, fix-and-flip, etc. Their goal is usually to maximize their short and or long-term profits.

Real estate investors need to understand when and where to buy investment properties. Understanding this requires them to have an in-depth knowledge of the real estate market. They need to know how to find the best investment properties for sale and analyze their profitability.

Passive real estate investors invest money in real estate without having much involvement in the day-to-day management of the real estate itself. Even if you do not have much money to invest, you can still become an investor in crowdfunded real estate investing projects.

For more information about this career path, you can visit:

- National Real Estate Investors Association - www.nationalreia.org

Real Estate Developer

Real estate developers typically buy raw land or land with teardown structure(s) and build one or more buildings on it. They can build any type of residential or commercial property (see Chapter 2 for a discussion of different types of properties) that are permitted given the zoning and entitlement efforts' success.

Real estate developers handle the financing, planning, and coordinating the construction of buildings. They put together a team to execute their plans. Real estate developers work with architects, engineers, contractors, listing agents and/or leasing agents, lawyers, and many other types of professionals.

There are no specific education requirements to become a real estate developer. However, it would help if you had a good grasp of the economy, the real estate market, the planning process, the construction process, and real estate finance.

For more information about this career path, you can visit:

- Commercial Real Estate Development Association - www.naiop.org

Real Estate Wholesaler

Real estate wholesalers perform the following activities:

- Look at distressed properties that are not currently listed for sale but whose owners are motivated to sell them quickly
- Determine current, in as-is condition property value
- Analyze the condition of the property and determine renovation costs and after repair value (ARV)
- Convince the property owners to sell the property to them and have them sign a contract
- Locate a buyer for the property (ideally, they should have buyers lined up by this stage)
- Sell the contract to the buyer or execute a double closing for-profit

The wholesaling strategy is different from the fix-and-flip strategy since, in wholesaling, no actual renovations are performed. If you think you will enjoy locating distressed properties and can convince people, this career path might be for you. You can start by getting a real estate license.

For more information about this career path, you can visit:

- National Real Estate Investors Association - www.nationalreia.org

Property Manager

Real Estate investors invest in residential and/or commercial properties. Many investors invest in rental properties but do not manage the properties themselves. Instead, they may hire a resident property manager, an on-site or off-site property manager/property management firm to take care of their investment(s).

As a property manager, you oversee the physical as well as the financial aspects of the property. You will work with both owner and tenant(s) to ensure their goals are satisfied.

Property management is covered in more detail in Chapter 14.

You can get started by getting your real estate agent license. For more information about this career path, you can visit:

- Institute of Real Estate Management - www.irem.org
- National Association of Residential Property Managers - www.narpm.org
- International Council of Shopping Centers - www.icsc.org

Home Inspector (Residential Inspector)

Real estate inspectors examine real estate for any defects or issues that will cause the buyer, seller, or agent problems. Inspections are a critical part of most real estate sale transactions. This is because home inspectors help point out any issues that might go unnoticed.

Home inspectors provide general inspections, including foundation, interior, electrical, heating and air conditioning, plumbing, roof, exterior, pool/spa, grounds, and parking structures.

Additional specialized inspections that can be performed include mold testing, chimney inspections, and sewer line inspections. Home inspections are discussed in more detail in Chapter 9.

Some states have licensing requirements for home inspectors. Other states do not. California, for example, does not currently have licensing requirements.

Home inspectors do need knowledge in many areas of home construction. Many organizations offer training specifically for home inspectors.

For more information about this career path, you can visit:

- American Society of Home Inspectors - www.ashi.org
- Check online for your specific state. For example, in California: California Real Estate Inspection Association - www.creia.org

Commercial Inspector

Commercial property inspectors are a critical part of most commercial real estate sales transactions. Commercial inspectors provide basic as well as optional specialized inspection services for commercial buildings, including retail, shopping centers, multifamily, warehouses, and the other commercial categories of real estate discussed in Chapter 2.

Commercial inspections are covered in more detail in Chapter 9.

For more information about this career path, you can visit:

- Certified Commercial Property Inspectors Association - www.ccpia.org

Real Estate Appraiser

Appraisers determine the value of residential or commercial real estate. They begin with gaining an understanding of the subject property's characteristics and location. They then compare the subject property to other similar properties that have recently sold and those currently available for sale. They adjust the comparable properties' prices and use those to establish a value for the subject property.

Private appraisers determine property values before they are sold or refinanced. Public appraisers work for governments to assess property values for tax purposes.

Residential appraisers determine the value of residential properties. Commercial appraisers determine the value of commercial properties. Appraising commercial properties is more complicated since many commercial properties are unique or have unique characteristics. This makes it more challenging to locate comparable commercial properties currently for sale or recently sold to establish value.

To become a real estate appraiser in California, for example, you need an appraiser's license. To get one, you need to complete appraiser education and pass a state exam. You should enjoy working with numbers and have the ability to handle many little details. Check online for the situation in your state.

For more information about this career path, you can visit:

- National Association of Real Estate Appraisers – www.narea-assoc.org
- American Society of Appraisers - www.appraisers.org
- Appraisal Institute - www.appraisalinstitute.org
- Check online for your specific state bureau. For example, in California: Bureau of Real Estate Appraisers - brea.ca.gov

Real Estate Loan Officer

Real estate loan officers help clients with obtaining loans to buy properties. Loan officers work for banks, credit unions, or other financial institutions. They assist borrowers throughout the application process for a mortgage.

Loan officers have knowledge of:

- Lending products and their characteristics
- Banking industry rules and regulations and their application
- Required documents for obtaining a loan and their handling

Loan officers pre-approve and verify the approval of prospective buyers. Loan officers should be well-versed in the various available loan programs, and the respective lender required repairs that would apply to those loan programs.

Loan officers should also offer listing agents a review of property condition before it is listed to advise them on any potential lender required repairs.

Loan officers must register with the Nationwide Mortgage Licensing System (NMLS). To register, you must meet specific qualifications. Real estate finance is discussed in more detail in Chapter 13.

For more information about this career path, you can visit:

- National Association of Mortgage Brokers - www.namb.org
- Mortgage Bankers Association - www.mba.org

Mortgage Broker

Mortgage brokers are intermediaries who bring mortgage borrowers and mortgage lenders together but do not use their own funds to originate mortgages. They help borrowers connect with lenders who represent the best fit for their financial situation and interest rate needs. Brokers also gather paperwork from borrowers and pass that paperwork along to mortgage lenders for underwriting and approval.

Mortgage brokers should be able to pre-approve or verify the approvals of prospective buyers of properties agents are selling.

Mortgage brokers need to be familiar with a range of mortgage products and advise customers on their availability, qualification requirements, interest rates, and terms. You should be good with numbers and people to be successful in this career.

Real estate finance is discussed in more detail later in the book in Chapter 13. For more information about this career path, you can visit:

- National Association of Mortgage Brokers - www.namb.org
- Mortgage Bankers Association – www.mba.org

Residential Mortgage Underwriter

Underwriters are experts that look at a borrower's finances and determine how much risk lenders take on if they decide to provide borrowers with loans.

Some of the things underwriters do include:

- Investigate borrowers' credit history, and search for late payments, bankruptcies, overuse of credit, etc.
- Order an appraisal to ensure that the amount that the lender offers for the home matches up with the home's actual value.
- Verify borrowers' income and employment.
- Look at the debt-to-income ratio (DTI) to ensure borrowers have sufficient cash flow to cover their monthly mortgage payments, taxes, and insurance.
- Verify borrowers' down payment and savings to ensure they have enough savings to use as a down payment at closing.

For more information about this career path, you can visit:

- National Association of Mortgage Underwriters - www.mortgage-underwriters.org

Commercial Mortgage Underwriter

Commercial underwriters review and recommend approval of commercial loans. Unlike residential underwriting, commercial underwriting of one asset may be very different than that of the next asset due to the wide range of commercial property types.

Commercial underwriters review many documents about the property, the market, the business entity seeking the loan, and its owners before making their recommendations.

For more information about this career path, you can visit:

- National Association of Mortgage Underwriters - www.mortgage-underwriters.org
- Commercial Real Estate Finance Council - www.crefc.org
- Mortgage Bankers Association – www.mba.org

Real Estate Asset Manager

Real estate asset managers are tasked with managing real estate assets, residential or commercial, for companies that own these assets.

They are typically employees. They may be responsible for acquisitions, property management, and/or disposition of assets. They typically work with real estate agents, property managers, and other industry professionals.

Foreclosure / REO Asset Manager

Foreclosure / REO Asset managers work for financial institutions, servicers, or asset management companies and help with the foreclosure and/or disposition of foreclosed assets. They need to be able to pay attention to many details, stay organized, and deadline oriented.

They sell some properties in their as-is condition mostly to investors, remodel others, and then sell to owner-occupants. They typically work with eviction attorneys, real estate agents, title specialists, and escrow officers to accomplish their goals.

Real Estate Attorney

In some states, real estate attorneys handle all related legal issues, including the transfer of title and mortgages.

Most residential real estate transactions in states like California are handled without a real estate attorney's direct involvement. However, attorneys provide advice to agents on an as-needed basis.

Attorneys often participate in more complex / larger scale residential purchases and commercial real estate transactions, including acquisition, disposition, development, leasing, and financing of real estate.

They work together with agents to structure complex sale or purchase deals. They can help with land use, permitting, and entitlements matters. They can help identify, evaluate, and resolve environmental issues. They can help with the various phases of more complex real estate development projects.

Real estate attorneys can also help with distressed real estate situations by acting quickly and strategically to preserve assets and resolve problems.

They accomplish this by:

- Negotiation
- Litigation
- Receivership
- Bankruptcy
- Mortgage forbearance
- Foreclosure

Some real estate attorneys handle a broad spectrum of areas of real estate, other practice in one or more areas, including:

- Landlord representation
- Evictions
- Tenant representation
- Real estate agent representation
- Foreclosure law
- Residential transactions
- Commercial transactions
- Litigation

To become a real estate attorney, you typically need a Bachelor's degree, you then need to pass the LSAT exam, You then apply for and complete a Juris Doctor degree, and finally, you need to pass your state's bar exam. You are also typically required to take Continuing Legal Education ("CLE") courses on an ongoing basis.

For more information about this career path, you can visit:

- American Bar Association – www.americanbar.org
- American College of Real Estate Lawyers - www.acrel.org
- Search online for your state's bar association. For example, in California: California Lawyers Association - www.calawyers.com
- Search online for county-specific bar associations – For example, Los Angeles County Bar Association -www.LACBA.org
- Search online for city-specific bar associations – For example, Beverly Hills Bar Association - www.bhba.org
- There are also more specialized bar associations – California Association of Black Lawyers - www.calblacklawyers.org

Real Estate Paralegal

Real estate paralegals help real estate attorneys. They may conduct title searches, prepare drafts of various real estate and real estate financing documentation. Real estate paralegals are not attorneys and must work under the direct supervision of.

For more information about this career path, you can visit:

- National Association of Legal Assistants – www.nala.org
- National Federation of Paralegal Associations – www.paralegals.org
- Search online for your state's paralegal association. For example, In California: California Alliance of Paralegal Associations – www.caparalegal.org

Escrow Officer

Escrow officers help facilitate the home buying and selling process. They work for escrow companies that are neutral third parties. Not all states handle the sale of real estate with escrow companies. Search the web to find out if this career applies in your state.

Once the process begins, documents and money are exchanged between the parties involved, and escrow companies facilitate this. Escrow companies maintain documents and funds during the closing process and until properties legally change hands. This includes the earnest money deposit (EMD), down payment, mortgage funds, as well as the title. Escrow officers facilitate communication among the various parties in the transaction.

They review the accepted offer and create a plan of action (known as escrow instructions). They have the title company run a title search to determine what needs to be done to provide the title insurance policy.

Next, they approach the lender(s) that provided financing to the current owner to determine how much they need to be paid (pay off demand). They also work with the new lender that will provide funds to help the buyer purchase the property to understand and comply with their requirements.

They receive funds from the buyer for the purchase of the property. They then prepare the deed and/or other documents. They prorate taxes, interest, insurance, and rents according to instructions.

They make sure all contingencies and/or other conditions are removed. They record the deed and any other relevant documents. Next, they have the title company issue the title insurance policy.

They disburse funds by paying off the seller's loans and paying real estate agents, vendors, title companies, and themselves. And finally, they prepare and provide final statements for the parties involved detailing how the funds were distributed.

For more information about this career path, you can visit:

- American Escrow Association – www.a-e-a.org
- Check online for your specific state associations. For example, in California: The California Escrow Association - www.ceaescrow.org

Title Representative

Title representatives investigate the status of a property's title to ensure that it is free of any obstacles that would interfere with the buyer's rights to the property and ensure that the real estate title is legitimately given to the buyer. Title representatives make sure that sellers have the right to sell the property to buyers.

Once title insurance companies do their verifications, they back these guarantees with title insurance, which protects lenders and/or owners in the event that someone comes along and makes a claim to the property in the future.

The title representatives perform research into public records related to the ownership history of properties. The results of such research are provided in the form of preliminary title reports. The reports provide all the parties to the transaction with information about the title's status on the property and conditions that need to be met for the title insurance to be provided.

Title representatives need to provide instructions for dealing with any outstanding mortgages, tax liens, or judgments on the property for the title insurance to be issued. Releases need to be provided by any parties holding a claim against the property. Title officers work to obtain these releases as part of the title search process.

Title representatives research ownership transfers to ensure they were recorded correctly. They also review liens to make sure they were property released at each ownership change. There should be no gaps between owners that are unaccounted for.

A gap in the title could indicate fraud or an error made by the recording department. Regardless, title representatives work to get the necessary documentation so the title insurance can be issued.

The preliminary report provides information found during a title search on the property being sold. If the buyer is getting a mortgage, the underwriter will review this report to ensure it meets the loan's title requirements.

Once all of the preliminary title report conditions have been met, the title insurance is issued and is paid for at closing.

For more information about this career path, you can visit:

- American Land Title Association – www.alta.org
- Check online for your specific state association. For example, in California: California Land Title Association – www.clta.org

Real Estate Marketing Specialist

Marketing specialists are responsible for planning and implementing marketing for real estate agents, brokers, and other real estate industry professionals. They can either be employed full or part-time or work on a contract basis.

Marketing specialists work to define target audiences and messages via various channels to showcase a person, company, product, service, and/or brand.

They may create digital content, develop printed materials, manage social media, create campaign emails, and more. By performing these activities, they also help generate leads.

They measure the success levels of their campaigns and adjust them as needed to optimize outcomes.

This career opportunity is excellent for creative people that would rather not interact with buyers and sellers.

For more information about this career path, you can visit:

- American Marketing Association - www.ama.org

Real Estate Educator / Coach

If you love real estate and educating others, you can pursue a real estate education career. Of course, having some real estate experience before educating others is incredibly beneficial!

For more information about this career path, you can visit:

- Real Estate Educators Association - www.reea.org

Licensed General Contractor

General contractors construct new buildings and other structures or renovate existing ones. They work with architects, engineers, specialized sub-contractors, and others. General contractors help agents estimate the cost of renovating properties so that they can make decisions if it makes financial sense to sell the properties as is or invest in their renovations before sale.

For more information about this career path, you can visit:

- Associated General Contractors of America - www.agc.org
- Check online for your specific state's contracting board. For example, in California: Contractors State License Board - www.cslb.ca.gov

Licensed Landscaping Contractor

Landscape contractors focus on the planning, construction, and possibly ongoing management of yards, gardens, outdoor areas. They focus on human benefit, look, safety, and environmental sustainability.

A simple green lawn or drought-tolerant landscaping (depending on the client's perspective) can make a massive difference in the resale value. A $5-$8k investment can at times yield $20-$40k or more in returns. For more upscale homes, vegetation that complements the neighborhood is critical to maximizing the sales price. An experienced landscaping contractor can make this happen.

For more information about this career path, you can visit:

- National Association of Landscape Professionals - www.landscapeprofessionals.org
- Check online for your specific state and local associations. For example, in California: California Landscape Contractors Association: www.clca.org

Professional Organizer

Professional organizers work with sellers to determine what should be placed in storage, what should be donated and where, what should be disposed of, and identify items that can be sold in an estate auction or estate sale. Organizers sort through the personal property, categorize it and label it.

Some organizers also specialize in document management. Such organizers might have a legal background to understand what type of documents to look for, what should be stored, and what should be disposed of. Additional details about organizing the content of properties are presented in Chapter 6.

For more information about this career path, you can visit:

- National Association of Productivity and Organizing Professionals - www.napo.net

Home Stager

Walking through an empty house makes it harder to connect to for many buyers. Home stagers help buyers imagine so that they are more likely to see themselves living in a home. Once buyers connect with a home, they are more likely to act quicker and pay more.

Stagers use various materials, furniture, and expert designer touch to make houses feel desirable.

Some staging companies maintain a large inventory of furniture, artwork, rugs, lighting, plants, and accessories. Experienced stagers are familiar with trends in different areas and will stage accordingly.

For more information about this career path, you can visit:

- Real Estate Staging Association - www.realestatestagingassociation.com
- International Association of Home Staging Professionals - www.iahsp.com

Termite and Pest Control Specialist

Professional termite and pest control specialists focus on inspecting, identifying, and eliminating pests such as ants, bees, cockroaches, flies, mosquitos, spiders, rats, termites, etc.

For more information about this career path, you can visit:

- National Pest Management Association – www.npmapestworld.org
- The Structural Pest Control Board (SPCB) - www.pestboard.ca.gov - is California's regulatory agency requiring ongoing training. Check your state to see if there is an equivalent agency.

Code Compliance Retrofitting Specialist

Code compliance retrofitting specialists are knowledgeable in state building codes and local county and city ordinances that mandate that specific safety and conservation measures are in place before the close of escrow of real property. There are specific code requirements that dictate what retrofitting is to be implemented. These ordinances address things like:

- Smoke detectors
- Carbon monoxide detectors
- Strapping and bracing for water heaters
- Sliding door impact hazard glazing film
- Automatic seismic gas shut-off valves (that turns off the gas in a 5.1 or greater earthquake)
- Water conservation devices such as high-efficiency toilets, showerheads, and faucet aerators

These specialists understand how compliance laws change from city to city and ensure that properties comply with the relevant ordinances before the close of escrow.

Real Estate Investment Analyst

Investment Analysts evaluate different acquisition opportunities as well as development opportunities and provide detailed reports to management. They consider marketing packages, operating memorandums, financial statements, rent rolls, and other documentation. They also create or request the creation of Broker Price Opinion and Opinion of Value reports.

They may also look at existing properties owned by their organizations to identify which ones are underperforming and should be restructured or disposed of.

It could be beneficial to study for and receive a real estate license to be better prepared for this career.

Real Estate Acquisitions Analyst

Acquisitions analysts focus primarily on evaluating acquisition opportunities and providing reports to Acquisition Managers. They may also get involved in a support role during the actual acquisition of the properties being purchased.

They look at properties available for sale on online platforms such as loopnet.com, and CoStar.com as well as off-market deals presented to them by real estate agents.

It could be beneficial to study for and receive a real estate license to be better prepared for this career.

Real Estate Dispositions Analyst

Disposition analysts focus primarily on evaluating disposition opportunities and providing reports to Disposition Managers. They may also get involved in a support role during the actual disposition of the properties being sold.

It could be beneficial to study for and receive a real estate license to be better prepared for this career.

Government / Real Estate Department Careers

There are numerous government jobs related to real estate. Real Estate Departments for various states have jobs associated with licensing, education, and code enforcement. They need examination proctors, investigators, supervisors, managers.

For more information about this career path, you can visit:

- Association of Real Estate License Law Officials – www.arello.org
- International Association of Assessing Officers – www.iaao.org
- National Association of Housing and Redevelopment Officials – www.nahro.org
- National Council of State Housing Agencies – www.ncsha.org

Urban Planning Careers

Urban planners work with local governments, civic groups, and private consulting firms to plan urban or suburban communities' future growth. They propose changes to accommodate this growth.

Urban planners develop plans and programs for the use of land. They use planning to create communities, accommodate growth, or revitalize physical facilities in towns, cities, and counties. Some universities offer degrees in urban planning.

For more information about this career path, you can visit:

- American Planning Association – www.planning.org
- Urban Land Institute – www.uli.org

Real Estate Research Careers

Real estate researchers help gather information and convert it to data and knowledge to benefit real estate decision-makers. Some look at the overall economy and its relationships to the real estate market. Others research specific cities, neighborhoods, or properties.

They may work for financial institutions, REITs, governments, and other organizations.

For more information about this career path, you can visit:

- Real Estate Research Institute – www.reri.org
- American Real Estate Society – www.aresnet.org

Part Two – Introduction to Real Estate Sales

Part two looks at what successful real estate agents do, from establishing property values to closing deals. Chapter 4 looks at valuation (pricing) of real estate. Chapter 5 looks at how agents handle occupied properties they list for sale. Chapter 6 looks at how agents handle vacant properties. Chapter 7 looks at what agents do to market properties. Chapter 8 looks at how agents manage offers. Chapter 9 looks at how agents handle closings (escrow).

This part of the book is laden with technical details and procedures. They are provided to you so you can determine if real estate sales are genuinely for you. If you find the particulars manageable and of interest to you, then you can use this portion of the book as a reference guide as you pursue this career. Much of the discussion in this part of the book is based on California real estate law and may or may not apply in your state.

Chapter 4 - Valuation of Real Estate

Chapter Overview

Chapter 4 looks at establishing a realistic value of a real estate asset you are handling. A property's value is a critical factor in establishing a property's list price prior to disposition. It is also important to establish value when helping with real estate acquisition to determine what maximum amount it makes sense to pay for properties.

This chapter looks at the components of a typical Broker Price Opinion (BPO) report for residential properties and a Broker Opinion of Value (BOV) report for commercial properties. It then discusses appraisals. The chapter concludes with discussions on establishing list prices for residential and commercial properties based on these reports.

Chapter Outline

Goals When Selling a Property

Broker Price Opinion (BPO)

Broker Price Opinion Components

What is a Comparable Property?

Broker Opinion of Value (BOV)

Appraisal

Establishing a List Price for Residential Properties

Establishing a List Price for Commercial Properties

Goals When Selling a Property

When selling a property (vacant or not) for a client, the goals typically include (see Figure 21):

- Maximizing returns
- Minimizing carrying costs
- Minimizing the chance of legal action taken against you due to errors you or your vendors make
- Minimizing tax liabilities

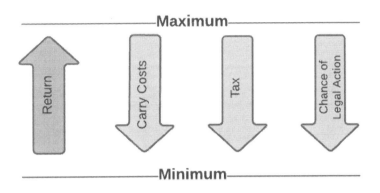

Figure 21 - Goals for Selling Properties

To achieve these primary goals, you should consider the issues discussed in this chapter.

Broker Price Opinion (BPO)

Price opinion reports, or Broker Price Opinion (BPOs), as they are often called, are beneficial to understand how to create and set you apart from most agents who do not wish to learn to create them and instead use automated tools to generate pricing reports.

It would be best if you learned to create custom pricing opinion reports. You can show them to your seller leads as a way to get them to list with you.

You can show them to your buyer leads as a way to recommend to them how much they should offer for a property they wish to purchase.

Broker Price Opinion Components

A typical report includes:

- Positive features of the subject property
- Positive features of the street and neighborhood
- Negative features of the subject property

- Negative features of the street and neighborhood
- 2-3 Sold comparables (comps)
- 2-3 Active listing comparables (comps)
- Analysis of how each Sold comp compares to the Subject property
- Analysis of how each Active listing comp compares to the Subject property
- Discussion of what the best Sold comp is and why
- Discussion of what the best Active listing comp is and why
- Any price adjustments based on the comps, and their positive and negative features relative to the Subject property
- The estimated cost of renovations (if there is interior access)
- Proposed list prices (as is, repaired)
- Likely sale prices (as is, repaired)

What is a Comparable Property?

A Comparable property is one that is similar in specific ways to a subject property and whose value is known. Identifying comparable properties helps estimate the list and sale price for your subject property.

Different people will provide you different perspectives, but most professionals would tell you this:

- A comparable property should ideally be within +/- 10% of the subject property's interior square footage. So, for example, if the subject property is 1,500 SF per title, the comps you search for should be between 1,350 to 1,650 SF (10% of 1,500 is 150 SF).
- A comparable property should have within +/- 1 bedroom of the subject. So if the subject property is a three-bedroom house, your comps should ideally also have three bedrooms, but no less than two bedrooms and no more than four bedrooms IF 3 bedroom homes are not available.
- A comparable property should have within +/-1 bathroom of the subject. So if the subject property has two bathrooms, ideally, your comps should also have two bathrooms but no less than one bathroom (obviously!) and no more than three bathrooms.
- A comparable property should be within a 0.25-mile radius of the subject property. If unable to find sufficient comps, you can expand to 0.5 miles or even a one-mile radius. The farther the properties are, the less likely they are to serve as reasonable comps. However, in rural areas, the search for comps can extend to 10 miles from the subject and beyond.
- A comparable property should be in a similar condition to the subject, if available, so if the subject is a heavy fixer, comparables should ideally be heavy fixers as well.
- A Comparable Sale should be one that took place within the past six months.

For condos, comparables should ideally be within the same complex and have the same number of bedrooms and bathrooms as does the subject property.

Broker Opinion of Value (BOV)

A BOV is very similar to a BPO. The term is primarily used for the valuation of commercial real estate assets by commercial agents. Commercial agents, for the most part, find their comps in CoStar.com

Loopnet.com data, which is publicly available, is not sufficient since it does not provide Sold property information needed to establish value.

CoStar has been and continues to be the authority in commercial data nationwide. Costar subscription cost is very high relative to MLS subscription, and most residential agents do not have access to Costar data.

Appraisal

Professional appraisers get their data from assessors and recorder's offices as well as other sources. They get to select comps just like agents do and can provide you with a value depending on your needs.

On many occasions, mortgage companies' appraisers appraise properties to the agreed purchase price. This allows these sales to go through.

Establishing a List Price for Residential Properties

Once you provide a BPO or BOV to your client and recommend a list price and a likely sale price, your client will need to determine the list price and then provide that to you.

Let's look at a few examples.

If three properties similar to the subject property sold for $300k, $315k, and $340k in the past three months within 0.25 miles of the subject. What should you list the property at? How much can you expect to receive for the property?

The answer depends on how quickly you want to get into escrow.

The lower your list price, the more likely you are to have more eyes look at the property, which is expected to result in more offers. If you are an aggressive negotiator, you might be able to push the offer amounts higher and higher.

Comparing based on price per SF is another way to arrive at a likely sale price for a property. Find Sold and Active comps, record their sold and list prices per SF and average them. Then, multiply these average prices per SF by the total SF of your subject property to arrive at the likely list and sale prices.

Ultimately, the most critical aspect of real estate sales is pricing. Properties sit on the market because the price is wrong. Properties move when they are priced correctly. Using the proper pricing strategy is critical in the real estate sales process. The correct strategy will generate the highest priced offer possible for the sale of your real estate asset.

Selecting a strategy depends on the location, a client's needs, local market conditions, and the overall economy. Three pricing strategy examples are discussed next.

First Pricing Strategy: For Ultra Luxury Properties

The segment of ultra-luxury properties exists in various markets throughout the country. It's all about location, location, location. The flats of Beverly Hills in the 90210 zip code, BHPO, Holmby Hills, Bel Air, Brentwood, and Pacific Palisades, have homes priced in the range of $5 to well over $40 million.

Most of the time, there's limited inventory for the entry-level homes in these neighborhoods. Therefore, rather than using a pricing strategy based on dollar per square foot, agents often list a $5 million property for substantially higher than the comparables, say for $7 million, to test the market for either owner-occupant or investor buyers who are hungry for these types of properties.

An investor will sometimes tear down the home, invest an additional $5 million to build a new home, and then sell it for over $20 million. If there is no buyer at $7 million, they may reduce the price by $500k - $1 million within a few weeks. Buyers love deals! Reducing the asking price by one million dollars is quite a deal and can generate lots of excitement!

Second Pricing Strategy: For Average Priced Properties with No Pressure to Sell Quickly

Another approach some agents utilize for average-priced assets in the $500k - $1 million range where there's a limited inventory of similar properties and the seller is not pressed for funds and is therefore not in a rush to sell, is to price the property a bit higher than the comparables.

If, for example, the pricing analysis based on sold and active comparables show that a property's current value is $700,000, agents offer the seller to list the property at $799,000 to test the market. If showing requests start pouring in as well as offers, they are in luck! Market conditions sometimes drastically change, and this works! However, suppose there is no activity and no showings. In that case, some agents encourage their clients to permit small and frequent price reductions, say of $20-$25k every two weeks until they hit a price point where activity is generated and showing requests are being made. If showings continue to occur, but there are no offers, they adjust the price reductions to $5-$10k every two weeks.

The goal is to identify the appropriate pricing point that generates significant buyer demand, resulting in lots of showings and a multiple offer situation, thereby further pushing the prices up by creating competition amongst the buyers.

Third Pricing Strategy: For Average Priced Properties with Pressure to Sell Quickly

In situations where the seller is pressed to sell quickly, some agents utilize this pricing strategy to create competition and excitement amongst buyers. The strategy applies to a real estate asset in the $500K - $1 million range. Using the same property as in the example above, if the pricing analysis based on sold and active comparables indicate the property's current value is $700,000, some agents may suggest to the seller to list the property at $649,900.

The goal is to take an aggressive approach towards pricing, very similar to the pricing set in an auction environment. Such an approach generates lots of interest from day one and creates a competitive environment among buyers. Agents let all buyers know that there's a multiple offer situation, apply aggressive yet delicate countering measures, and push the prices up as high as is possible.

When a property is placed on the market well below the pricing of comparables, there's a considerable level of interest. This most often generates a multiple offer situation, which pushes the sales price to higher than market value! This strategy gets similar results as you would in an auction environment.

Establishing a List Price for Commercial Properties

Commercial valuations are generally more complex than residential valuations. This is the case since values are often dependent upon elements like:

- Current market rents
- Fewer available comparables
- Maintenance costs (which can differ significantly from industry to industry)
- How much are buyers willing to pay (there are usually fewer of them than for a typical residential deal).

With many variables to consider, how do agents price a commercial property? You can use any of the five real estate valuation methods to determine commercial properties' values (see Figure 22).

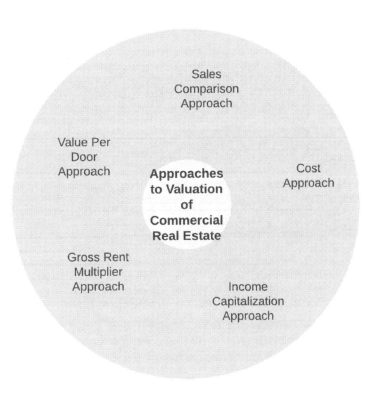

Figure 22 - Approaches to Valuation of Commercial Real Estate

Sales Comparison Approach

This valuation method is based on recent sales data for comparable properties (recently sold buildings with similar characteristics from the same market area).

For example, an industrial warehouse might be compared to another sold in the same area during the past few months. It is often difficult to find recent comparables for similar properties since there are far fewer commercial properties to start with, many of whom are unique.

Cost Approach

This valuation method incorporates the cost to rebuild an equivalent structure, accounting for the current cost of associated land, construction materials, construction labor, and other expenses related to replacing the existing structure.

The cost approach is generally applied when comparable properties are hard to find, such as when the property has relatively unique or specialized improvements or when the upgraded structure(s) add substantial value to the underlying land.

Income Capitalization Approach

This valuation method is based on the income an investor can expect to generate from a particular property. That projected income is derived from a comparison of other similar local properties.

Investors use capitalization rate analysis to determine the most they can pay for an income-producing property based upon the net income and a rate of return.

The property value is calculated by dividing the Net Operating Income (NOI) by a desired or expected rate of return (Cap Rate).

Property value = NOI/Cap

Let's look at several examples. If a property is generating a net operating income of $80,000 annually and the Cap rates in the neighborhood for this type of property are 4%, then the property value is about $80,000 / 0.04= $ 2,000,000.

You can look at this differently: if a property with an $80,000 NOI is selling for $2,000,000, then the Cap on this deal is 4%.

Say a building is purchased for $10 million, and the current net income is $500,000. The in-place Cap rate is, therefore, 5%. Say you believe that you can increase the net income by replacing some tenants with higher-paying ones and/or decrease the costs, thus increasing the net income by $100,000 to $600,000. This provides you a potential (Pro-Forma) Cap rate of 6%.

Now, say a building generates a net income of $500,000 per year, and the Cap rate in the area is 5%. How much can you expect to receive for the sale of the building? The answer is $10 million.

Gross Rent Multiplier Approach

The Gross Rent Multiplier (GRM) takes the property's purchase price and divides it by its gross income. For example, if you purchased a commercial property for $1,000,000 and it generates $160,000 in gross rents each year, your Gross Rent Multiplier would be $1,000,000 / $160,000 or 6.25. This method is typically used to identify properties with a low price relative to their market-based potential income.

Now, say that properties are selling at 6.25 percent GRM in a particular area. If the property's annual gross income is $160,000, then you can expect to receive $1 million for the sale of this property.

Value Per Door Approach

This commercial real estate valuation method is used primarily for apartment buildings. This method simply determines the entire building's value based on the number of units. A building with 20 apartments priced at $4 million, for example, would be valued at $200,000 "per door" regardless of each unit's size. Buyers know the maximum "price per door" they are willing to pay in a given area and will not look further into buildings that are substantially overpriced per door.

Now, say your building in the same area has 30 units. Given the $200,000 price per door, you could expect to receive $6 million for the sale of this property.

In the end, every seller, buyer, and agent values property differently. The valuation of commercial property relies heavily on numbers but also has a large subjective component.

Chapter 5 - Handling Occupied Properties

Chapter Overview

Chapter 5 provides a perspective on handling the disposition of occupied properties in situations where the occupants' presence reduces the likely sale price substantially.

It looks at possible issues with occupied properties. The chapter then discusses relocation assistance, the eviction process, and the handling of abandoned personal property. It is based on current California law, so you should check with an attorney how this works in your state.

Chapter Outline

About Handling Occupied Properties

Issues with Occupied Properties

Relocation Assistance

The Eviction Process

Handling Abandoned Personal Property after Termination of Tenancy

About Handling Occupied Properties

Most of the time, you will be selling properties that are either vacant or have paying tenants that are generating income for the properties.

From time to time, agents are asked to sell properties that are occupied with no apparent access. Many of them list these properties on the MLS as Occupied and sell them to investors at a substantially discounted price.

Experienced and caring agents take the extra time and handle occupied properties in a way that can yield the maximum return on the sale of each asset.

The information provided in this chapter is not intended to be a substitute for legal advice in any specific tenancy or unlawful detainer action. And, it is assumed that you have the legal authority to sell the subject property.

The process outlined is based on California law at the time of writing this book. You should consult an attorney as laws may change at any time, and of course, they may be different in your state.

Issues with Occupied Properties

From time to time, agents encounter issues when selling occupied properties. The more common ones include rent control, rekey, non-payment of rent, no access, and illegal units (see Figure 23 below).

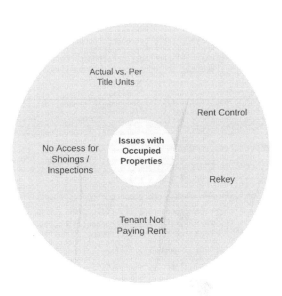

Figure 23 - Key Issues with Occupied Properties

In many situations, you might be selling a single-family home or condo, you are familiar with the tenant and/or know if they are paying rent and how much. This, however, is not always the case, and at times you may not be aware of the actual situation with the tenants.

The first step for you is to establish a clear and comprehensive understanding of the situation. This can be accomplished by asking the following questions:

What kind of property is it? Residential? Commercial? How many units? You should look at the title, as well as visit the property and perform a visual inspection.

Legal/Illegal Units

Are all units legal? If not, how many are illegal? That would be the difference between the number of units on title and the number of the actual units or addresses utilized/affixed.

How many units are tenant-occupied at the property? If you do not know with certainty, you should knock on the exterior doors of the property. To confirm, check with neighbors. Ensure you are aware of the title-holder name or names to cross-reference with additional/different names.

Rent Control?

Is the property rent-controlled? You should check and confirm with the city, which will usually provide that information via telephone or online.

Unit Information

For each occupied unit, determine:

- Is the tenant paying rent?
- What is the current rent?
- Is there an operative lease governing the tenancy?
- What is the remaining term of the lease? Obtain a copy of the lease.
- Is the unit rented month-to-month?
- How does the unit's rent compare to fair market rent value for similar units in the subject's vicinity?

If the documentation is up to date and available, then you have the answers. Otherwise, you could request, on the seller's behalf, that each tenant complete a Tenant Estoppel. An Estoppel is a certified statement by a tenant that verifies the terms and conditions and current status of their lease. It confirms the occupant's understanding and expectations of their respective lease terms.

No Access – No Showings?

Some agents have been led to believe that if a property is occupied with no contact with the tenant(s), then the property should be sold without providing interior access to investors (usually for a substantially lower amount than fair market value). You should make an effort and work with the tenant(s) to provide access. This could be a selling point for you, the agent that wishes to distinguish themselves from the competition in such situations.

Tenant Not Paying Rent?

Your seller has a right to issue a Three-Day Notice to Pay or Quit once a tenant is one or more days late paying rent and the available paperwork has established a tenancy. The notice should be delivered in person, possibly by you. If the tenant does not open the door, you should post it to the front door with tape and take a date stamped photo for your records. If the tenant does not pay rent within three days, your seller has a right to start eviction proceedings against this tenant. Consult with an evictions legal professional on how to proceed.

Entering Occupied Properties with a Non-Cooperating Tenant?

A seller has a general right to enter the premises to show it to prospective buyers, provided reasonable notice, which would typically be upon 24 hours of written notice to enter. If no access is provided, eviction proceedings may be appropriate. Before undertaking a potentially lengthy and costly process such as an eviction, you might consider providing the occupant with relocation assistance to leave asap. Relocation assistance and evictions are discussed in the following sections.

Relocation Assistance

Relocation Assistance, also known as Cash for Keys (CFK), is a procedure where a property owner offers its occupant to vacate by a specific date in exchange for an agreed-upon amount of money. The occupant(s) must sign a Cash for Keys Agreement, and the contract specifies the move out date and the cash for keys amount. It also specifies that the occupant(s) will not damage the property. The cost to repair any damage, along with the cost of any unpaid utility bills, will be deducted from their Cash for Keys amount.

The contract also specifies that the occupant(s) will leave the property clean, both interior and exterior, in "broom swept" condition on the move out date. It also specifies that the property owner has the right to bring an unlawful detainer (eviction) action against any occupant who does not vacate after the specified move out date.

The occupants agree to cooperate and allow access for showings of the property to prospective buyer(s) or tenant(s). The contract also specifies that occupant(s) waive their rights to any minimum notice to end the occupancy, usually provided by the owner before proceeding with an eviction.

All adult occupants must sign the agreement, and by signing, each occupant holds harmless and releases the owner and their agents from any action related to the property.

Before offering a Cash for Keys amount to an occupant, you should consult with an eviction attorney to determine the current state and local requirements. You will need first to determine if state rent control laws govern the property. As of the writing of this book, in California, it applies to multifamily properties that are over 15 years old or a condo or single-family residences that are owned by corporations or real estate investment trusts. Duplexes where the owner lives in one of the units, are exempt. You should check the situation in your state if you live outside of California.

Next, you should check to see which city the property is located in or if it's located within an unincorporated area of a county. If the city where the property is located has rent control, it will have specific requirements on Cash for Keys amounts. If the property is located in an unincorporated area within the county, if there is rent control at the county level, find the required amount for CFK from the county. If there is no rent control, the owner can offer any negotiated amount to the occupant.

It would be best if you handled Cash for Keys for your clients as a first step to try to avoid evictions. There many success stories where a few thousand dollars was motivating enough to a non-paying tenant to move out in 30-45 days and leave the property in "broom swept condition". That's a great deal for the seller, given how expensive trash outs can be. Per the agreement, the property must be delivered free of trash and personal property, both inside the property, the exterior, and any detached structures such as sheds and/or garages.

Some agents handle the entire process - from reaching out to the occupant to getting the CFK agreement negotiated and executed, meeting the occupant at the property to conduct a walkthrough, and providing the occupant with payment (provided to you by the owner).

It may take some time to establish rapport with the occupant, take time to listen to their story, exhibit empathy for their situations, and share this great opportunity with them. A real estate agent with the right personality traits will skillfully negotiate a Cash for Keys on behalf of the owner and save them time and money while building their own reputation in the industry.

The Eviction Process

An understanding of the eviction (unlawful detainer) process is essential for any property owner, agent, or property manager. The following is a basic description of the residential eviction process in California (See Figure 24). While you can have the seller hire an eviction attorney, it is still essential to understand this chapter so that you can oversee their work by asking the right questions throughout the process.

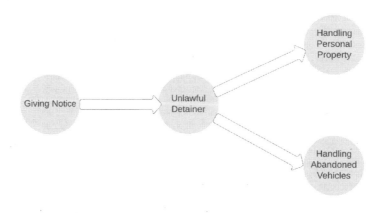

Figure 24 – A bird's Eye View of the Eviction Process

Giving Notice

Your seller may evict a tenant who refuses to pay rent or abide by the terms of the lease agreement. It is necessary to obtain a judgment and writ of possession from a court of law before evicting the tenant. This form of a court proceeding is referred to as an unlawful detainer action. Common situations where the seller might initiate unlawful detainer actions include:

- To terminate a periodic tenancy (where the lease has no end date)
- The tenant fails to pay rent
- The tenant has violated the lease agreement in some other way

If your seller cannot reach a satisfactory solution with the tenant, they should consider giving the required notice and initiating an unlawful detainer action (consult an eviction attorney).

Since eviction is an expedited court process that causes tenants to forfeit their rights, you must comply with procedures.

Unlawful Detainer Action

An unlawful detainer action is appropriate only after the underlying tenancy is properly terminated. This typically involves giving the tenant some form of notice. Either a three-day, 30-day, 60-day, or 90-day notice is used to terminate a tenancy.

Terminating a Tenancy

The landlord/tenant relationship (tenancy) is created by contract and/or operable law. If the tenant stops paying rent or breaches the rental/lease agreement in another way, the seller can terminate the tenancy.

A seller cannot terminate a fixed-term lease before the lease expires unless the tenant fails to pay rent or violates the lease agreement in some other way.

A month-to-month tenancy continues until either the seller or the tenant terminates the tenancy with proper written notice (see below).

Types of Notices to Tenant

There are different types of notices: "three-day," "30-day," and "60-day" notice. Under some circumstances, a seller may have to provide a "90-day" notice, such as when the tenant is under the Section 8 program, under rent control, or pursuant to applicable "foreclosed-tenant" statutes.

Using a Three-Day Notice

Three-day notices are commonly used when:

- The tenant did not pay rent - The tenant receives a "three-day notice to pay rent or quit." The notice gives the tenant three days to either pay the rent (and stay) or

leave. California Association of Realtors (C.A.R.) form PRQ (Notice to Pay Rent or Quit) may be used for this.
- The tenant violates the lease agreement in another way - The tenant receives a "three-day notice to perform covenant or quit." The notice also gives the tenant three days to perform the covenant (e.g., ensure that no pets are on the premises) according to the lease agreement (and stay) or leave. C.A.R. form PCQ (Notice to Perform Covenant (Cure) or Quit) can be used for this.
- The tenant commits violations that are not curable and/or are serious. For example, Waste (destroying the property), Illegal activity, Nuisance (for example, continuous loud music after repeated warnings), Illegal sublet (against the terms of the lease). The tenant receives a "three-day notice to quit." This notice is unconditional. It means "get out within three days.". C.A.R. form NTQ (Notice to Quit) may be used for this purpose.

Serving a Three-Day Notice

You or your seller can deliver a copy of the three-day notice in person. If the tenant is not available, you should post the notice at the property (and take a date stamped photo).

The day of service of a three-day notice is counted as day zero. The next day after the day of service is counted as day one. Weekends, legal holidays, and "court holidays" (when courts are closed) are not counted as part of the three-day period.

Accepting Rent within the Three-Day Notice Period

If the tenant offers to pay the full rent amount within three days of receiving the notice to pay rent or quit, you must accept the payment, and the tenant may remain in possession.

However, if the tenant offers partial payment, you can refuse to accept and continue the eviction process. Acceptance of partial payment can invalidate a three-day notice. This rule relates to residential tenancies, not commercial tenancies where partial payments might be acceptable under certain circumstances.

If the rent is not paid within three days or if your seller refuses to accept a partial payment, and the tenant does not vacate the premises, your seller can then file an unlawful detainer action to terminate the tenancy and recover possession.

Using a 30-day or 60-day notice

If a tenant has resided at the property for less than one year, the thirty-day notice is usually used to terminate a month-to-month tenancy.

If a tenant has resided at the property for one year or more, you should usually provide a sixty-day notice to terminate a month-to-month tenancy. C.A.R. form NTT (Notice of Termination of Tenancy) may be used for this purpose.

Exception to the 60-day Notice

There is an exception when a month to month tenant has lived in the property for more than a year. The seller need only give a 30-day notice to terminate if ALL six of the following criteria are met:

- The seller has entered into a contract to sell the property to a natural person(s).
- The purchaser intends to reside in the premises for at least one year following the termination of tenancy.
- The landlord has established an escrow with an escrow company licensed by the Department of Corporations or a licensed Real Estate Broker.
- The escrow was opened 120 days or less prior to the delivery of the notice.
- The title to the premises is separately alienable from any other dwelling unit (i.e., a single-family unit or condominium).
- The tenant has not previously been given a notice of termination of tenancy.

As long as all six of the above criteria have been met, then even a month-to-month tenant that has been in the property for more than a year may be given a 30-day notice to terminate the tenancy. See section 3 of C.A.R. form NTT.

A tenant's fixed-term lease expires, but the tenant refuses to move

If the tenant's fixed-term lease expires, but the tenant refuses to move out, your seller can proceed with the unlawful detainer action. The lease agreement provides the tenant with notice of termination of the tenancy. While formal notice may not be required if the requirement for such is not specified in the lease, you should, however, inform the tenant in writing at least 30 days before their lease expiration date and indicate that there will be no renewal of the lease or any continuation of the tenancy. You can use C.A.R. "Lease Expiration Letter".

The Unlawful Detainer Action

Filing the Unlawful Detainer Action

After serving the tenant with notice, you must allow the appropriate notice period (i.e., 3, 30, 60, or 90 days) to pass. When the notice period passes, the Unlawful Detainer (UD) action can be filed in court, and the summons and complaint can be served upon the tenant.

Absent enumerated exceptions, you must attach specified documents to the UD complaint in residential eviction complaints, including a copy of the lease agreement, the notice of termination, and a "Proof of Service" indicating how the notice of termination was served. The complaint must also be "verified" (signed by your seller under penalty of perjury).

The procedure for evicting

After the tenant is personally served with the UD complaint, the tenant has five days to respond. Other forms of service may dictate different allowable response periods.

If no answer is filed, your seller may file for a "default judgment" immediately without going to court for a hearing. The clerk will then issue a "writ" for possession, directing the Sheriff to proceed with the eviction. Once issued, a sheriff can post a notice providing the tenant five days to vacate.

If the tenant challenges the eviction, then a court date will be set (usually three weeks after the answer is filed). Assuming your seller wins, the judge will sign an Order granting possession and/or a monetary award for damages, after which a "writ" for possession, directing the Sheriff to proceed with eviction, can be issued. As with a default, a sheriff can then post notice giving the tenant a final five days to vacate.

Length of an Unlawful Detainer Lawsuit

Adding the steps previously discussed typically takes between one to three months to obtain a court judgment for possession. A "contested" eviction where the tenant files an answer will require two to three months. An uncontested eviction where the landlord can take a default judgment will be in the one to two-month range.

Removing a tenant once a Judgement is Obtained

As mentioned, once your seller obtains a judgment against the tenant, they can request that the court clerk issue a writ of possession. You or your seller should then deliver the writ of possession to the local county marshal or sheriff's office and request that the marshal or sheriff evict the tenant, also known as a "lock-out".

The marshal or sheriff will then notify the tenant that they have five days to remove their personal property and vacate the premises. If the tenant does not leave within this time, the marshal or sheriff will physically remove the tenant after notifying you of a date and time of a "lockout" (the tenant is NOT notified) from the premises and restore possession to the landlord. The landlord will be allowed to change the locks at that time.

Handling Squatters

You or your seller should contact the local police and seek their assistance. The police should be willing to assist you so long as the squatters concede that they were not given lawful possession. However, if they claim they have a legal right (for example, an alleged oral agreement with the owner), the police might not remove them from the premises. Instead, a court order may be required.

To remove unwilling squatters, you should make a demand that they leave the premises. California law has a provision that may apply to squatters, where, after a five-day notice, the owner can proceed with a "Forcible Detainer" action rather than unlawful detainer action.

A forcible detainer action involves different rules and procedures. It may not apply to every squatter situation, where an Unlawful Detainer or another legal method may be utilized to evict the squatters. You should seek legal advice before deciding the most suitable approach to evict squatters if the police are unwilling to remove them from the property.

Handling Abandoned Personal Property after Termination of Tenancy

When you dispose of personal property left behind after a tenant has vacated, the California Civil Code provides an optional procedure as well as forms to clarify the rights of the tenant and the landlord.

These forms and the procedure can, with slight differences, be used for both commercial and residential tenancies. You can provide your seller with these forms. One for residential tenants called "Abandoned Personal Property (Residential) Letter" and one for commercial tenants called "Abandoned Personal Property (Commercial) Letter." Following the proper procedures will help to protect you and your seller legally.

Landlord's Request that Tenant Retrieve Property (Residential)

If a tenant leaves personal property at the property at the termination of the tenancy and the tenant has vacated, you or your seller should provide the tenant a notice in writing to inform them that the property left behind should be retrieved or otherwise it will be sold or disposed of in accordance with the law.

You or your seller must give written notice to the tenant and any other person the seller reasonably believes may own the property. If the property consists of records, the tenant shall be presumed to be the owner of the records.

If possession was granted to the owner by way of a court order and through the execution of a writ of possession by the Sheriff, the above notices are not necessary as such notice is included as part of the writ of possession served/posted by the Sheriff as part of the eviction process.

Delivering the Notice

You or your seller can deliver the notice to the tenant by email, personal delivery, or first-class mail to the owner's last known address.

Format of Notice

The notice must comply substantially with the format of the forms presented in the California Civil Code. One notice would go to the tenant and the other to someone other than the tenant if the seller believes someone else to be the personal property owner.

You can provide your seller with the "Abandoned Personal Property (Residential) Letter" (Sample Letter form "APPR").

The C.A.R. Sample Letter form is only for the person who is the tenant. It is not for someone other than the tenant where the seller believes that person to be the personal property owner.

Storing Abandoned Property

The personal property which the seller has described in the notice must either be left at the vacated premises or stored by the seller in a safe place until the seller either releases the property to the tenant or rightful owner or disposes of the property at a public sale.

Releasing Abandoned Property

A seller may release the property to a former tenant or to any other person the seller reasonably believes to be the owner of the property as long as the tenant or other owner pays the reasonable storage fees and takes the personal property before the date specified in the written notice.

It is advisable to obtain the written declaration of the person claiming to be the owner as to their ownership of the personal property and the basis of their right to reclaim the property. This can protect the seller if some other claimant later alleges that the property was released to the wrong person. At all times, the owner must remember to act reasonably, making decisions that would answer the question of a judge or jury: "was it reasonable to believe that the person was the owner of the released property?"

Conducting a Public Sale of Personal Property

First, the seller must wait until the date to claim property given in the notice has elapsed.

Then, a notice of the public sale's time and place must be published in a newspaper in the county where the sale is to be held (Notice of Sale).

Handling Sale Proceeds

The seller can deduct the reasonable expenses for storage, advertising, and sale from the sale proceeds. If not claimed, the balance must be paid into the county's treasury in which the sale took place not more than 30 days after the sale.

The seller may refer to the property owner to the county treasurer. The property owner has one year from the date of sale to file a claim to the treasurer for the balance of the sale proceeds.

Handling Abandoned Vehicles

Almost all municipalities have their own rules, regulations, and ordinances governing the disposition of abandoned vehicles. At all times, all such local statutes and regulations must be reviewed carefully for compliance.

Chapter 6 - Handling Vacant Properties

Chapter Overview

It is vital to make sure the property is secured and, if not, take appropriate actions to secure it. A decision needs to be made if to sell the property as-is or renovate it. Actions need to be taken to preserve the condition of the property. Hazards and vandalism need to be handled if encountered.

Chapter Outline

Is the Property Secure?

As-Is vs. Renovate

Property Preservation

Hazards

Vandalism

Is the Property Secure?

The goal is to minimize the chance of vandalism, occupancy by squatters, or others that are not meant to be at the property.

You or your seller should secure the property if it is not secure. In addition to having a locksmith rekey the doors, some companies specialize in securing vacant properties with a variety of technologies from metal screens to plastic screens for doors and windows (if the home is in a higher crime area and/or you feel it could use extra security, or you have had prior illegal occupancy of the property).

Security guard services are a more expensive solution suggested for specific high valued residential properties or certain commercial properties.

As-Is vs. Renovate

You should be flexible to handle the property the way your seller believes it should be handled. Sometimes that means selling the property as-is, and sometimes it means renovating before the sale to maximize the return on the sale.

You should be able to provide your seller with a cost-benefit analysis of various scenarios to determine the best strategy for the asset. Possible scenarios are (see Figure 25):

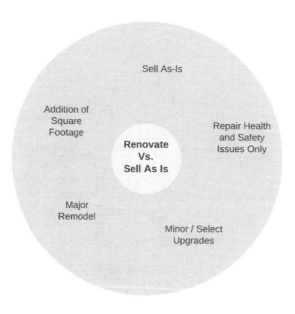

Figure 25 - Renovate vs. Sell As-Is

- **Sell As-Is** – depending on the current property condition and property location, it may appeal to owner-occupants, investors, or both in its current, as-is condition. In areas where there is "mansionization", it does not make economic sense to do a major

remodel since these properties are in high demand by investors looking to tear down and rebuild to maximize the return.
- **Repairs** - to address health and safety issues only, to allow for purchase by owner-occupants.
- **Minor upgrades** - such as interior paint or a new roof.
- **Major remodel** - including new floors, paint, upgraded bathrooms, and kitchen with new appliances.
- **Addition of square footage** - adding square footage to properties in locations where the $/SF is high will maximize the return on the asset. Consider, for example, a two-story property on a slope in Beverly Hills 90210, where the upper floor is finished and previously occupied, and a 1,000 SF walk-out basement is unfinished. Finishing the walk-out basement at the cost of $200,000 will allow you to sell the property for an ADDITIONAL $1,000,000!

It is known that investors purchase fixers to fix and flip or to fix and hold. Investors make their buying decisions based on their analysis and desired return, and therefore expect to acquire the property at a discount below market value.

Sell As-Is

If the property is in good condition, then selling as is, of course, is the way to go.

In many cases, it may not be immediately apparent if it is better to sell as-is or embark on renovations. Therefore, you should provide an analysis of various scenarios. You would need to have the interior of the property inspected, take photos, consult with your contractors, and use the gathered information for your report.

You could also have the property inspected by a professional home inspector, request the necessary repair bids, and prepare a report that shows a cost-benefit analysis, which includes required and as-is comparables.

Selling as-is, in most cases, still requires a comprehensive sales clean. In many situations, it is recommended to remove existing personal property, followed by a professional sales clean and, depending on the property's location, a professional staging.

What does it mean to sell a property in "As-Is" condition? At the close of escrow, the buyer is purchasing the property in its existing condition on the date of acceptance. The seller is not obligated to repair defects that exist as of that date. The seller does, however, have to disclose known material defects. The seller is also responsible for maintaining the property in the condition it was in on the date of acceptance. As-Is does not mean you take the property as you find it on the date of close of escrow, but instead, the condition it was in on the date of acceptance. The buyer can determine the condition by reviewing the seller's disclosures and making an independent investigation of the property to discover its actual condition.

Repair the Basics – Health and Safety Issues – Required by Lenders

Another approach is to fix the basics – the health and safety issues required by lenders.

Examples of health and safety issues are missing or non-operating smoke and/or carbon monoxide detectors, missing flooring in living spaces, dry rot, roof shingles missing, missing water heater straps.

Renovate

The scope of a renovation should conform to the neighborhood. You should analyze if currently listed or pending properties and recently sold properties (go back 12 months) have been renovated just before their sale. If so, you should determine which standard they were renovated to (types of materials, colors, layouts) and make an appropriate recommendation.

An experienced contractor should identify the same and recommend materials, appliance brands/models that fit the neighborhood, and ensure the property is renovated without being under-improved or over-improved for the area.

Does it "Make Sense" to Renovate?

"Make sense" is often used in the real estate and construction industries to mean "profitable".

To determine if it would be profitable to renovate a property, you should provide your client with an analysis of properties in the same area. Some of these properties should be of similar "fixer" condition of the subject (average sold fixer price "AFP"). Some of these properties should be "ARP" (average sold repaired price "ARP"). Carrying costs for the duration of renovations ("CC"). Cost of repairs ("CR"). The amount of profit or loss due to renovation is, therefore, calculated as follows:

ARP- AFP-CR-CC = Amount of profit or loss due to renovation

This calculation will allow you to make a better decision. For example, if you can sell a fixer property for $450,000 or renovate at $600,000, will you renovate? Let's say it takes two months to renovate, and it costs $65,000 to renovate and carry costs for two months total of $5,000. Does it make sense to renovate?

$600,000 − $450,000 − $65,000 − $5,000 = $80,000 would be the likely additional profit due to the renovation. It would make sense to proceed with such a renovation unless home prices are rapidly declining to offset such gains.

Property Preservation

There are multiple property preservation activities that you could handle on your seller's behalf, depending on your workload and other considerations. These activities include (see Figure 26):

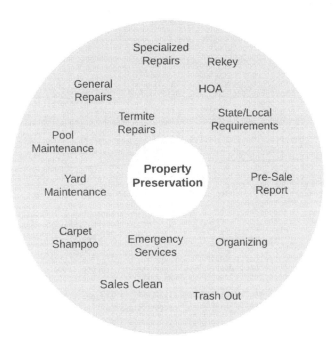

Figure 26 - Property Preservation Categories

Rekey

Determine the number of exterior doors at the property.

You can have the locksmith install a lockbox at the property in a location of your choosing and have two keys placed inside. You can take one and keep it once you visit the property, so you have an extra copy.

It is best to install the lockbox in a hidden location, behind foliage, or on a water pipe.

If a property has an attached garage, there is no need to rekey any garage doors if interior access is available from the house's interior and the garage door is secured.

If a property has a detached garage, the garage entrance is also rekeyed to the same key code as the front door. Appraisers, inspectors, and buyer's agents require access to all areas of a property to complete their investigations.

HOA Services and Amenities

HOAs sometimes take care of certain or all utilities at a property and usually handle yard maintenance and common areas' maintenance.

It is essential to conduct your due diligence and determine which amenities the HOA offers and if the HOA handles payment for any utilities. This information is used for marketing the property, as buyers usually want to know what their monthly HOA fee will pay for. Buyers of properties with HOA usually compare amenities among associations.

Common amenities include a community pool, fitness room, conference room, playground, security services, and more. The monthly HOA fee is usually used to pay for some of the utilities, maintenance of the grounds, and the common amenities.

HOA FHA Approval

An HOA must be FHA approved for the property to qualify for an FHA loan. You may determine if the HOA is FHA approved by checking the HUD website (currently https://entp.hud.gov/idapp/html/condlook.cfm). If an HOA is not FHA approved, the inability to obtain FHA financing may impact the property's marketability and therefore value, so you should consider this when completing the Broker Price Opinion.

The HOA's reserve levels and delinquency rates may affect the property's value. Suppose an HOA suffers from a high delinquency rate (many owners are not paying their dues). In that case, lenders may not have confidence in their ability to make necessary insurance payments and repairs to the property and common areas. Similarly, low reserves also mean a question about the HOA's ability to fulfill these responsibilities.

Reserve levels and delinquency rates are used as some of the loan qualification criteria by lenders and may result in a lender not approving the loan.

State and Local Retrofitting Requirements

The transfer upon sale of a property often requires that specific state and county or city provisions are met. These items often include retrofitting repairs, inspections, or ordering reports to buyers to ensure the property meets local (such as the Department of Building and Safety) and state legal requirements.

To determine which requirements apply to a property, you should check with the local building and safety or housing department.

If the property is located within an incorporated city, reach out to the city's building and safety department. If it's located in an unincorporated portion, the county's retrofitting requirements will apply. The state's retrofitting requirements must be adhered to in each situation. In California, the state requirements are identical to those of Los Angeles County requirements, for example.

If the city or county indicates that a pre-sale report or pre-sale inspection is needed, this should be handled immediately. Often, city inspectors are back-logged and may not be able to process the application or visit the property for weeks. If these items are not handled as early as possible, they may cause delays to the close of escrow.

Some local requirements cannot be handled until the property is in escrow (for instance, a buyer's signature is required). In those instances, as much of the process that can be handled should be done as soon as possible, and the rest are put on hold until you can complete it.

Re-Inspections

If the city inspector or code enforcement officer identified any items requiring correction that are not being assumed by the buyer, a re-inspection after the work to remedy is completed is usually needed to resolve the issue. Other re-inspection types include final inspections after all permits are filed, and work is completed.

It is crucial to schedule re-inspections as soon as possible to prevent delays to the sale of the subject property.

Organizing the Content of a Property

When selling real property that contains personal property, you might consider utilizing a professional organizer's services. An experienced organizer can provide you with the following services:

- Cataloging with photos or making an inventory list of the personal property
- Labeling and sorting items, either to be disposed of, donated, stored, or sold.
- Selling items at an estate sale at the property or online.
- Working with specialized estate sale vendors and auction houses to determine what could be auctioned through them.
- Packing and organizing personal property going to each of the destinations: off-site storage, donation, auction house or estate sale vendors, and trashout.
- Coordinating the services of trashout vendors, auction houses, and estate sale vendors.

Trashout

A trashout is the removal of all trash from inside and outside of the property, including detached structure(s). The California Residential Purchase Agreement states, "all debris and personal property not included in the sale, shall be removed by Close of Escrow". Unless this is negotiated out of the contract during the offer negotiations process, the seller must complete the trashout. In addition, the property will be more marketable and will allow for a greater return on the sale of the property. This must be completed before a sales clean and carpet shampoo.

Sales Clean

A sales clean is the thorough cleaning of the property's interior to ensure potential buyers will find a clean and fresh-smelling property upon their visit. Often air fresheners are recommended to give the property a "home" feel.

Initially, the property should get a deep cleaning and include cleaning windows, window sills, baseboards, inside and outside kitchen appliances, cabinets, the kitchen, bathrooms, dust, and clean floor surfaces, mirrors, and fixtures.

A sales clean could be repeated if the property is still on the market 2-3 months after the initial sales clean. A follow-up sales clean can be a basic cleaning that's lighter, not a deep cleaning.

A good sales clean requires water and electricity, so utilities should be on at this point.

Carpet Shampoo

Carpet shampooing is an essential step in preparing a property for showing. Flooring occupies significant viewable space in a property, so unpleasant floors can turn off buyers from an otherwise attractive property. If a full carpet replacement is not needed, then a carpet shampoo is probably a good idea.

A carpet shampoo is merely using a machine to shampoo (the machine shampoos, rinses, and extracts the water as it's pushed along) all carpets to prepare the home for showings.

If the carpet is old and worn, check to see if there are hardwood floors underneath and get a bid to remove the carpets instead. Removing the carpets would make the property more marketable.

Yard Maintenance – Initial and Ongoing

Initial yard cleaning should include trimming trees and/or bushes. Ongoing maintenance should, at a minimum, include grass trimming on a weekly or bi-weekly basis.

The initial yard service can cost as little as what an ongoing service would cost, up to hundreds of dollars, depending upon the yard's size and condition. If CFK vacated a property, there might not be much to do. If it has been vacant for a long time due to the decedent passing away at a facility and no one maintained the property, there might be tall grass and significant overgrowth. The initial service must include pruning, trimming overgrowth, and removal of debris, in addition to the routine requirements outlined below.

Continuing lawn maintenance is required while the property is vacant. It is also necessary if the property is occupied by a tenant who is unwilling to maintain the yard. Local city officials will often issue citations for properties that are not being maintained. Unkempt yards also act as a sign to others that a property is vacant, which may attract vandalism and squatters.

The landscaping must be neatly trimmed, adequately watered, and free of debris and unsightly weeds. It is important to follow local and regional rules about water use (days and times when watering yards are allowed). Failure to observe these requirements may result in fines issued to your seller and not the offending vendor.

Even properties without yards or with dirt lots must be maintained, as there is more to ongoing maintenance than just a trim and mow—debris must be cleared, sidewalks swept, newspapers removed, the property inspected, etc. Establishing an expectation that the vendor briefly inspect the property during their visits and provide any necessary feedback (note graffiti, broken windows, leaks, etc.) is hugely beneficial.

Pool Maintenance – Initial and Ongoing

Pool maintenance is required for all properties with a pool. You may decide to either keep the pool filled, fill the pool if empty, or drain the pool - a drained pool is considered less of a maintenance liability but a greater safety liability. A filled pool makes the property more marketable and is safer.

If the pool is to be drained, the contractor must be sure to follow all local guidelines and avoid draining into the property yard if at all possible.

If the pool must be cleaned, it must be filled with water and managed with chemicals (or for saltwater pools, with salt) regularly. The pool's pumping and filter systems must also be periodically inspected during these ongoing maintenance visits to ensure proper operation and cleanliness. The pool surface needs to be skimmed to maintain an attractive appearance and prevent any clogs to the pool's pump and filtration system.

In either case, the pool area must have locked gates or a pool cover, and the locks must be changed as part of the initial rekey. Securing/installing the gate or pool cover is a requirement of the initial pool service. Fence and cover requirements are often mutually dictated by your seller and the subject's city, county, and/or state.

Any local requirements must take priority. Requirements often include cover type (mesh vs. wire), fence, gate height, method of securing, and established weight tolerance. Subsequent maintenance services must include inspections of all locks, gates, and covers to ensure they remain secure.

If there is damage to the pool, the lining of the pool, or the pool's filter system, appropriate repairs can be requested and made. A specialized vendor is recommended for pool repairs, though an experienced general contractor may also complete them satisfactorily.

Ongoing maintenance service visits are essential and easy opportunities for the property to be inspected. Establishing an expectation that the vendor briefly inspect the property on these visits and provide any necessary feedback (note graffiti, broken windows, leaks, etc.) is extremely beneficial.

General Repairs

Most services that do not fall in the categories mentioned above are considered general repairs—painting, wall repairs, carpet replacement, replacing broken windows, repairing leaky faucets, etc. More specialized general repairs will be discussed in the following sections.

Suppose you decide to renovate a property instead of selling it as is. In that case, it is essential to obtain general repair bids as early as possible to be utilized in pricing opinions.

A general contractor should be used when a general repair bid is needed. Some general contractors have specialties, such as flooring, retrofitting, plumbing, etc. If multiple contractors are available, the contractors for the relevant work should be requested to provide bids. For some services, such as HVAC or termite repairs, a specialized vendor is usually preferable to a contractor with only limited experience with such work.

Most repair requests made during the marketing or escrow periods, such as lender-required repairs, emergency repairs, leak repairs, vandalism, etc., fall under general repairs. You must maintain a reliable relationship with multiple contractors so that these items may be addressed reliably and promptly.

Termite Repairs

Termite repairs are specialized repairs meant to eliminate wood-destroying pests or rot and replace damaged structural elements to maintain their integrity.

The report will come back, showing that either the property is free and clear or that termites, rot, fungus, or other problems were found. Some items will be listed as **Section I** repairs, and others in **Section II**. Section I items are areas of evident infestation or infection, and Section II items are areas likely to lead to infestation or infection, such as a pile of wood. Many lenders require that all Section I items be repaired. Having those items addressed is also considered part of making a property move-in ready.

Termite repairs may be authorized by your seller or required by the buyer or buyer's lender during the closing period. Either way, repairs will need to be completed as soon as possible, as delays may impact the property's sale timeline. Depending on the scope of repairs taken, additional steps may be necessary to ensure the safety of all parties who may visit the property and limit the seller's liability.

Sometimes a termite report will come back stating that repairs must be made by a licensed contractor other than the termite company. These usually include replacing major wood sections of a property, such as stairs, fencing, patio covers, and window frames.

Once all termite repairs are completed for either Section I or Section I and II, the termite vendor should be asked to provide termite clearance. This document states that they certify the property to be free and clear of existing wood-destroying pests and often includes a warranty to address any items discovered over the following year or more. Any lenders requiring termite repairs usually require the clearance stating that they were completed.

Specialized Repairs

Certain repairs may require specialists to bid on, as a general contractor may lack the expertise to provide a reliably comprehensive bid. The most significant risk is that the general contractor will not be aware of all building code or permit requirements related to certain repair types, which may create liability for the seller or future homeowner once repairs are completed.

Providing quality repairs is essential, and using a specialized vendor often offers higher quality and longer-lasting repairs for certain repair types. The trade-off, of course, is that specialized vendors usually cost more than general contractors.

The most common types of specialized repairs include termite repairs (as discussed earlier), septic or well system repairs, roof repairs (though general contractors are often certified in roof repairs or have sufficient experience with them), foundation repairs, and well repairs.

Emergency Services

Emergency services are repairs that need to be handled quickly, as damage and liability often increase the longer the service is delayed. Each situation must be handled individually based on particular circumstances.

- **Gas leaks** – Call your local gas company asap

- **Water leaks** – If a shut-off doesn't suffice at stopping the leak, then minimal contractor services may be needed. Bringing fans to dry damage or pump water out may be necessary.
- **Broken windows** – If the window is prominent, a contractor may need to be hired to board up the window.
- **Broken doors** - If the door has street access, a contractor may need to be hired to install a new deadbolt or board up the door.

In other words: the property must be secure and safe at all times, and matters that may exacerbate (gas and water leaks) should be handled before they become larger issues.

Hazards

Hazards are environmental issues that affect the safety of individuals entering a property and may pose a risk to the subject property itself. The three most common types of hazards are fire damage, flood damage, and mold damage.

Hazards may affect a property without notice. They may be caused by malice, weather, negligence, breaks, appliance malfunction, and more. If no one is at the property to identify these issues early, they can snowball and become more extensive. Because of this, regular inspections and the recruitment of the neighbors' watchful eyes are highly recommended.

Mold Damage

Dark blotches usually found in bathrooms and kitchens, though possibly found anywhere, are usually signs of mold. Mold is a common blight in vacant properties as stagnant water, slow drips, and leaks contribute to the wet and humid environments that mold favors. Not only unattractive to potential buyers, but mold can also present a health and safety risk. Your seller needs to decide if to sell the property as-is or handle mold remediation before having you begin to market the property.

Any indication that there may be mold or mildew is often referred to as "signs of discoloration.".

All environmental reports, including mold inspection reports, must be provided to the buyer as part of the customary disclosure of property condition.

Beneath the kitchen sink, tile grout, bathroom ceilings, and behind washing machines are all common locations to find discoloration signs. Leaks from pipes, in the roof, or the exterior walls may cause large mold problems as insulation and drywall material becomes wet. Given its thickness and absorbency, insulation can harbor large amounts of mold that may cause a noticeable odor upon entry to the property.

Small traces of mold or mildew can usually be remedied with the sales clean. As this will likely not eliminate all spores, any history of discoloration should still be disclosed by you with the property condition disclosure.

If mold damage is significant—your guidelines maybe along the lines of 100 contiguous square inches—then a waiver may be required for anyone, including vendors, who wish to visit the property before the mold is abated. If a property is not being sold As-Is and will be renovated, bids from a mold specialist will be required to address the issue. Once treatments and repairs are made, access without waivers may be permitted.

Bids to correct the mold source should be provided by general contractors who are more experienced with general repairs. Abating the mold but not correcting the source is only a short-term solution.

Fire Damage

Fires can very quickly and very seriously damage property. As most sellers have insurance for their assets, with coverage against fire damage, they will need a fire damage report to file a claim.

A fire inspector or other representative of the local fire department or the fire department that extinguished the fire can provide the fire damage report. Typically, these reports include:

- The known or suspected cause of the fire
- A general description of the damage caused by the fire
- An opinion as to the integrity of the property's structure based on the damage sustained

Based on the inspection, the inspector may tag the property to restrict access. Any access restrictions should be noted. If any work to correct the issues to the property is completed. In that case, a new inspection from the fire department will be needed to update any tags and allow for regular occupancy of the property.

As ash and smoke will linger in a property for an extended period, the low air quality may be a health risk to anyone who enters the property. Also, the fire may damage the property's structure in a manner that makes it possible for debris to fall from overhead.

Because of these risks, only insured vendors who acknowledge the risks and individuals who sign a hold harmless should be allowed access to the property. If there is any concern that the whole structure's integrity is unreliable and may collapse, no one should be allowed entry.

When the property is listed, MLS remarks should indicate there is restricted access, and no lockbox information should be provided. Buyers' agents should be instructed to email the listing agent. Once the buyers' agents and buyers have signed the hold harmless, access information can be provided. Still, language should be added, stating that access is only offered to the specific people listed. Property entry requirements should be posted on the front door, indicating a mask must be worn when entering.

If you wish to consider repairing the property, then bids should be requested. The seller can usually use insurance proceeds to pay for these repairs. Typically there are extra permits needed to correct fire damage that would not otherwise be required. Even if repairs make a property look like the fire never happened, it still must be disclosed to any buyers to limit liability.

Flood Damage

Multiple sources can cause flood damage:

- Broken pipes
- Poor drainage
- Clogged rain gutters
- Malfunctioning appliances
- Roof leaks
- Heavy rains and runoff
- Forgetfulness

Once flooding is discovered, steps should be taken immediately to remedy the situation. Simply opening all doors after water levels outside have receded will let out much of the water. Pumps should also be used. For smaller amounts of water, canister vacuums (large barrel vacuums with no bags) are effective.

Large fans should be used to dry carpet and walls to salvage them and prevent mold or mildew growth (discoloration). Pulling up the carpet can be effective in allowing the padding beneath to dry more quickly as it increases the surface area exposed to the dry air. If salvageable, Carpet can later be reset, though the water may have caused it to shrink. New paint is often needed to cover water stains.

If discoloration is present, a specialist may be needed to determine the full scope. The specialist may have tools to heat the studs in the walls to prevent them from retaining water for an extended period and contributing to fungus, rot, or mold (usually, these boards only soak up enough water for this to be a threat if their exposure is prolonged).

Like any other damages, all flood damages need to be disclosed to buyers, even if the damage is not evident after drying or repairs.

Vandalism

Vandalism is when an act is committed against the subject property in a manner that affects it negatively. Vandalism effects can sometimes reduce the property's value.

Vacant properties are not only more susceptible to vandalism—they're often easy targets that provide utility services and blank walls—but the lack of periodic inspections means that vandalism is more likely to go unseen long enough to bring about more damage.

You should inform your seller of each incidence of vandalism at a property. The three key categories of vandalism are:

Squatting

Vacant properties are susceptible to unauthorized entry and indefinite habitation by persons, usually vagrants. This is known as squatting, whereby the individual occupies the property to stay there as long as possible.

They usually treat the property with little regard while inhabiting it, which means even a short stay can lead to expensive damages.

Theft of water heaters and other appliances is common for such properties. Squatters may also revisit properties sporadically, including during marketing times. Such situations often mean spooked buyers who lose interest in a property.

If a lockout has been conducted at a property, it is easy to clear it of any squatters. The lockout documents can be provided as proof that no one is supposed to occupy the property. The police will enforce that by removing whoever is inside the property.

In other cases, whether or not the squatters can be easily forced out depends upon whether or not they claim the right to occupy the property. If they do, the police officer or sheriff will make a judgment of their claims, erring on the side of caution. If the individual may be telling the truth, they will usually request that you procure a court order. If they do not believe the squatter, they will force them out.

Multiple entries are not uncommon. All sources of entry and other possible sources of access must be secured.

It is considered a violation if a vacant property is occupied by a squatter in some cities, with responsibility going to the property owner for imprudent action. Fines or additional property security requirements may be imposed. For the latter, if the property owner does not comply with the requirements, the city may complete them and place a lien for the cost against the property, plus additional fees.

Therefore, it is vital to conduct regular property inspections, especially in areas with higher squatting instances, larger vagrant populations, or near heavily traveled roads. Any cases of squatting should be disclosed to prospective buyers.

Dumping

Dumping is the intentional placement of trash or unwanted personal property on the subject property to avoid the financial or time burden of proper disposal. Often, it is neighbors who commit the act, knowing that the property is vacant. Commonly dumped items are usually bulky furniture such as sofas and mattresses or old inoperable appliances. Simple bags of trash are not uncommon.

In cities with vacant property ordinances and areas governed by HOAs or PUDs, property owners who fail to clean up trash dumped on their property can face fines and liens if the city officials or HOA-hired vendors eventually complete the work. Once again, it is vital to conduct regular inspections to identify whether trash has been dumped at a property to be removed promptly.

Your vendors should inform you of any dumping instances, and these should be disclosed to your seller and prospective buyers.

Graffiti

Graffiti is not limited to spray-painted gang names—it includes any unauthorized defacement of property surfaces. The most commonly occurring graffiti is "tagging"—marking property with a gang name or symbol with paint, marker, or another, usually permanent, medium.

In most major cities, the responsibility to remove or cover graffiti lies with the property owner. Sometimes deadlines are as little as 24 hours. If graffiti is painted over, it should be—in some cities, must be—painted with a color matching the subject's existing paint.

Frequent property inspections allow identifying graffiti before a city abatement crew addresses it, and a lien is placed against the property. If a property is regularly subjected to tagging, the police department should be notified. If they believe it to be a marker of high gang activity in the area, they will increase patrols to discourage such activity. Any instances of graffiti should be disclosed to your seller and prospective buyers.

Chapter 7 – Marketing Properties

Chapter Overview

Chapter 7 provides a survey of the activities involved in marketing properties. It covers signage at the property, professional photos, videos, 3D tours, property description, and property website. The chapter then discusses placing the property on various online listing services, making it available to other agents and the public in general. It concludes with a look at open houses, showing properties and price reductions.

Chapter Outline

Signage

Professional Photos of Property

Property Description

Professional Video and 3D Virtual Tour

Professional Website

Placing the property on the MLS, LoopNet, and CoStar

Traditional Marketing

Online Marketing

Conducting Open Houses

Showing Properties

Handling Price Reductions

Marketing Activities

You should complete a listing agreement and have your seller sign it (ideally electronically) before you proceed to list and market the property.

Once you establish a price for the property, the pre-marketing activities have been completed or are in progress, and the listing agreement is signed, you will proceed with marketing the property. Marketing activities should include the following (Figure 27):

Figure 27 - Real Estate Marketing Activities

Signage

You should place a sign at the property. Standard signs in Los Angeles, for example, are 2'x3' on an 8 ft post. However, some cities or HOAs have different sign requirements or no signs allowed. You should confirm with the city and/or HOA to ensure the correct signs are installed to avoid fines that you may need to pay if a sign does not conform to the requirements.

Professional Photos of Property

You should hire a professional photographer to take interior and exterior photos of the property for marketing purposes. There is no excuse not to take professional photos of a property. Professional photos increase the marketability of the property and make you look good!

Photos should be taken once the property interior and exterior have been cleaned up and ready for sale (unless circumstances do not permit cleanup, such as if the property is tenant occupied).

In situations when interior access is not possible, the professional photographer should take exterior photos only.

Professional Video and 3D Virtual Tour

A professional video is appropriate for most properties to increase the online visibility of the property.

Types of videos:

- A video that combines a series of photos with background music
- A video tour where you are walking the property and showcasing it
- A virtual 3D tour such as a MatterPort (matterport.com)

Property Description

The property description should showcase the property in a positive light without going overboard. The description should list the property's positive features and indicate if it is a fixer or not.

The following is an example of a professional description for a property for sale: "Beautiful move-in ready Country Club Estates single level ranch style home with gorgeous hardwood floors throughout has three bedrooms and two and a half baths and is on one of the most desirable streets in Beverly Hills. Spacious rooms with a generous kitchen with granite countertops and a center island with wine storage and newer appliances. Vaulted ceiling with a built-in entertainment system and cozy fireplace in the living room. The skylit dining room and living room with french doors lead to the backyard with a built-in spa and waterfall, adding a magical charm to this home. The master suite includes a sitting area, marble remodeled full bathroom, soaking tub and separate shower, walk-in closet, and french doors that lead to the large patio area and lushly landscaped yard that includes a BBQ."

Professional Website

A professional website is appropriate for high valued properties (that are not fixers), typically for luxury properties. The website should include the following components:

- Main photo
- Additional photos
- Key features
- Description
- Video(s)
- 3D Tour
- Your contact information

Placing the property on the MLS, LoopNet, and CoStar

You should place the property on the local MLS. If the property is commercial, you should place it on the local MLS, as well as on LoopNet and CoStar.

The listing should include professional photos, a video of the property, and a link to the property website (for high valued properties).

Another benefit of placing the property on the MLS is that it automatically propagates to Zillow and 100+ other websites that buyers are likely to search, and therefore increase its online visibility.

It is essential to place your residential properties on the MLS and the commercial properties on Loopnet and CoStar since it allows for maximum property exposure to agents and the relevant buyer pool.

Many agents set up their buyer clients with automated email notifications for properties that match their search criteria. This means that when a property comes on the market and matches the buyer's search criteria, the buyer receives an automated email from the MLS with the property details.

Traditional Marketing

You should create a property flyer. You may request to review and approve it. You should place several color property flyers at the property, possibly on the kitchen counter.

There are other traditional marketing channels, such as ads in local papers, magazines. Note that most buyers are looking online, so for the most part, the primary beneficiary of such marketing is the agent and not the property.

Online Marketing

You should do the following to market your property online:

You should add the property to your website since some agents and buyers are likely to visit the website.

You should email about the property to your network of agents database. Each time an agent inquires about one of your listings, add them to your database, and over the years, you will end up with an extensive database of agents.

You should email about the property to your real estate buyers database. Each time a buyer reaches out to you directly, add them to your buyers' database, then email buyers that reached out to you over the past 12 months about your listings as they come on the market. If the buyer has identified themselves as an investor or inquired about an investment property, you should keep them indefinitely in your buyers' database.

You should also post about the new property on social media (LinkedIn, Facebook, and other platforms you use).

Conducting Open Houses

You should conduct at least one, but ideally, more than one open house and/or virtual open house to allow for buyers and other agents the opportunity to view the property.

Each open house should be advertised on the MLS (from there, it is propagated to Zillow and other real estate websites).

Showing Properties

Occupied properties should never have a lockbox installed for security and privacy reasons. Showings should be by appointment only.

You should insist that buyers are accompanied by their agents during showings of occupied properties. Vacant properties can have lock boxes installed. Lockbox access should be provided to buyer's agents.

Handling Price Reductions

Most properties, in most conditions, have a price at which one or more buyers will buy them. In most cases, there is no good reason for a property to sit on the market for a lengthy period.

If the property is overpriced, you should report to your seller the level of activity on the property and suggest a price reduction to the seller. You should explain to the seller why you are making the request, the reduction amount proposed, and provide supporting data such as comparables.

If the seller approves the price reduction, you should send your seller a new listing agreement to sign, reflecting the new listing price.

Chapter 8 – Managing Offers

Chapter Overview

Chapter 8 presents the steps agents take to handle incoming offers for the purchase of their listings. It looks at the basic components of an offer package, including the state purchase contract, proof of funds, pre-approval letter, and additional components that apply depending on the situation.

The chapter then covers presenting offers to sellers, selection of offers, countering, and negotiation strategies.

The chapter concludes with a discussion about assembling the contract package, getting it signed by the parties to the contract, and distributing it.

Chapter Outline

The Offer Management Process

Receiving Offers from Buyers / Their agents

Basic Components of a Complete Offer Package

State Purchase Contract/Purchase Agreement

Proof of Funds (POF)

Loan Pre-Approval Letter (PAL)

Additional Components of a Complete Offer Package

Presenting Offers

Full Disclosure to Potential buyers

Selecting Offers

Countering Offers

When to Use a Counter and When to Use an Addendum

Assembling the Contract Package

Receiving, Reviewing, and Executing the Contract Package

Sending the Fully Executed Contract to the Buyer's Agent

The Offer Management Process

From the moment an offer is received to the moment escrow is opened, you will have much you are responsible for. Your responsibilities relating to the management of offers are discussed. The offer management process is shown in Figure 28 below and described in this chapter.

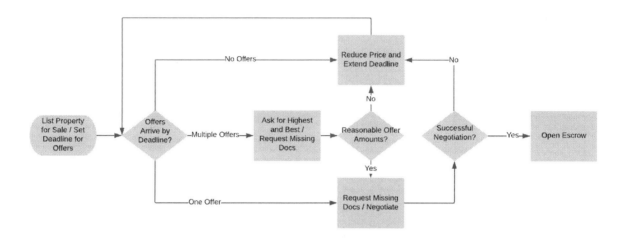

Figure 28 - Overview of the Offer Management Process

Receiving Offers from Buyers / Their agents

When a buyer's agent submits an offer package, you should ensure that the offer package is complete before presenting it to your seller. However, you should inform your seller via email as soon as offers start coming in and should advise of the offer submission deadline that had been set.

In this section, you will learn what constitutes a complete offer package and how to evaluate each component to determine whether supplemental documentation is needed.

If an offer package is incomplete or if the documents provided have been filled in incorrectly, you should request missing documents and/or revisions from the buyer's agent.

Basic Components of a Complete Offer Package

The basic components of an offer package and optional components (which apply to some situations only) are presented in Figure 29 below.

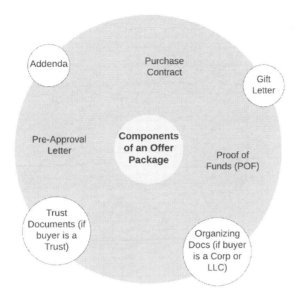

Figure 29 - Components of an Offer Package

Mandatory components:

- State Purchase Contract/Purchase Agreement and relevant addendums and advisories
- Proof of Funds (POF)
- Loan Pre-Approval Letter (PAL), if applicable

Optional components:

- Organizing documents (if the buyer is a corporation, LLC, etc.).
- Trust documents (if the buyer is a trust).
- Addenda
- Gift letter

The following sections elaborate on the above offer package components.

State Purchase Contract/Purchase Agreement

This document is the offer for a property. It is a contract that includes all of the buyer's requested terms, among other contractual terms.

The contract includes four contingencies, whose time periods begin on the first calendar day following acceptance. They are (see Figure 30):

Figure 30 - The Four Contingencies in the State Purchase Contract / Purchase Agreement

- **Inspection contingency** – a specified period allowing the buyer to conduct inspections and investigations of the property and provides the buyer the right to cancel the transaction and receive the deposit back if not satisfied with the inspection.
- **Title contingency** – the buyer has a specified amount of time to review the preliminary title report ("Preliminary Report") of the property. It allows the buyer to cancel the transaction and receive the deposit back if the buyer finds issues in the Preliminary Report that the buyer is not satisfied with.
- **Appraisal contingency** – a specified period of time, allowing a buyer who is obtaining financing for the property's purchase to obtain an appraisal. If the appraised value is less than the purchase price, the buyer has the right to cancel the transaction and get the deposit back. The buyer can still obtain financing if the appraisal value is lower than the purchase price. The buyer would have to make a larger down payment to make up for the difference.
- **Loan contingency** – a specified period allowing a buyer to apply for a loan to purchase the property. It provides the buyer the right to cancel the transaction and get the deposit back if the buyer cannot obtain financing.

You should ensure that all pages of the contracts are provided to you, completed as necessary, and includes buyer and buyer's agent's signatures and initials.

Acceptance date, or contract date, is defined as when communication of the final acceptance is made. It's the date when the offer or final counter offer is accepted in writing by one and is delivered to and received by the other party. If, for example, the seller accepts a buyer's counter offer and signs it, the "acceptance date" is not when the seller signs but when the buyer or buyer's agent receives the offer signed by the seller.

Proof of Funds (POF)

The buyer's agent must provide proof of funds dated within the past 30 days, showing the buyer's name on the account, and have sufficient funds to make the purchase.

Types of proof of funds include:

- Bank statements.
- Portfolio summaries reasonably in excess of the down payment. The buyer should have enough money to support the offer even if their portfolio's value drops unexpectedly.
- Funds from escrow if the buyer is currently in escrow and selling another property. In this case, buyer may provide a copy of the settlement statement.
- Cashier's checks.
- A letter from a bank or other financial institution indicating the amount of funds available and signed by an authorized representative. Verify whether the funds are cash or a line of credit.

If proof of funds is provided from a person other than the buyer's name, you should notify the buyer's agent and request proof of funds specifying the buyer's name or a gift letter if a gift is being provided. If the buyer's agent provides a gift letter, you should ensure that adequate proof of funds is still provided.

If the proof of funds specifies an entity's name, you should request organizing documents (see below). If proof of funds is listed under a trust, you should request trust documents or a gift letter (see below).

Loan Pre-Approval Letter (PAL)

If the buyer's offer is financed, the buyer's agent must provide a Loan Pre-Approval Letter (PAL) with their offer package.

You should review the PAL to ensure that the purchase price, loan amount, financing type, and occupancy type (investor or owner-occupied) is consistent with the offer contract. The PAL must also be dated within the past 30 days and list the buyer's name – indicating loan pre-approval for the buyer.

While buyers may still have their lender fund their offer, you may request a PAL from a trusted lender to double-check the buyer's qualification and prevent an escrow fallout.

Additional Components of a Complete Offer Package

After reviewing the basic components of an offer package, you may realize that additional documents are needed to supplement the offer. Each offer package must be reviewed to determine whether additional documents are required. The additional components that may be necessary are: Gift Letter, Organizing Documents, Trust Documents, Addenda.

Gift Letter (If Applicable)

If a person other than the buyer will be providing funds for the purchase as a gift, the offer package must include a gift letter. The gift letter explains that the buyer will be receiving funds for the purchase from another individual.

The gift letter must state the name of the individual providing funds, the amount of funds that will be gifted, the name of the person receiving funds, and the nature of their relationship. Contact information should be provided for both individuals, and both individuals must sign this document. Note that the person gifting funds still needs to provide adequate proof of funds for the offer.

Organizing Documents (if the Buyer is an Entity)

If the buyer is an entity, or if an entity is providing POF for an offer, the buyer's agent must provide the entity's organizing documents.

Organizing documents are written instruments by which the entity is created under state law. They show the names of the people who have the authority to sign for the company and a list of the company's principal owners, including each owner's percentage of ownership. The person signing offer documents on behalf of the company or LLC should be listed in the organizing documents.

Examples of organizing documents include Articles of Incorporation if the company is incorporated, Articles of Organization if it is an LLC and others.

Trust Documents (if the buyer is a Trust)

If the buyer is a trust or if a trust is providing funds for an offer, the buyer's agent must provide trust documents.

Trust documents are similar to organizing documents in that they show the names of those who are authorized to sign for the trust. The person signing offer documents on behalf of a trust should be listed as one of these individuals. All trusts must maintain these documents and should have a copy on file.

Addenda (If Applicable)

Various types of addenda may be included with a state purchase contract. These include: Addenda specified within the State Purchase Contract/Purchase Agreement and Addenda created after an offer has been submitted. The following sections elaborate on these addenda.

Addenda Specified in the State Purchase Contract

Some state purchase contracts have an area where the buyer's agent can specify the names of specific addenda to include with the offer package. Review the state purchase contract/purchase agreement to ensure that the buyer's agent has provided any additional addenda indicated in the contract.

Examples of addenda specifically outlined in the state purchase contract/purchase agreement for California include:

- Addendum # (CAR form ADM)
- Court Confirmation Addendum (CAR form CCA)
- Septic, Well and Property Monument Addendum (C.A.R. Form SWPI)
- Back-Up Offer Addendum (CAR form BUO)

Note: Addenda may still be included with the offer package, even if the addendum's name is not specified in the state contract.

Addenda That Are Created After a buyer Has Submitted an Offer Package, Prior to Final Acceptance

If any changes are being made to the state purchase contract after a buyer's agent has already submitted an offer, the change must be made in an Addendum. This most commonly occurs when the Highest and Best is requested (more will be explained about the Highest and Best later).

After offers have been presented to you, any terms that are negotiated between you and the buyer must be included in either a Counter or Addendum for it to be added to the state purchase contract (more will be explained about documenting negotiations later).

- **Counter** – used to reject existing term(s) and propose different term(s) with which to substitute the rejected terms.
- **Addendum** – used to provide an extension of the counter if there is no more space on the counter form, to reject terms and propose substitute terms.

Presenting Offers

If the price is right, there will be multiple showing requests during the first few days, and unless the description is not in line with reality, offers should start coming in.

In this case, offers should not be presented as they arrive. Instead, you should reach out to your seller, explain the situation, and suggest a deadline for offers.

You should make sure each offer package is complete, and if it is not, request missing documentation/information.

Once the offer submission deadline has passed, you should make sure all offers received are complete packages before submitting them to your seller.

You should provide to your seller, via email, three things:

- Attached offers
- A summary table with all offers
- A recommendation of which offer to select, why, and a proposal of how to respond to the offers

If only one offer arrives, you should go back to all buyer's agents who inquired about the property but have not submitted an offer. Let them know there is now an offer and give them an informal 24-hour deadline to submit their own offer if they are interested.

If there is more than one offer, a Seller Multiple Counter Offer should be issued requesting the buyer's Highest and Best purchase price and other terms.

Full Disclosure to Potential buyers

Sellers in California are required to provide multiple disclosures during escrow. Sellers have a duty to disclose to buyers all material conditions, defects, and /or issues known to them that might impact the property's value or desirability. Failure to provide disclosures could lead to a lawsuit.

If there are any issues with the property that is likely to affect the buyer's interest in the property or their offer price, you must provide the buyers' agents of all interested buyers the disclosure regarding the material condition of the property as soon as the offer is received. In California, probate, trust, bankruptcy, and REO transactions require that the seller complete the Exempt Seller Disclosure ("ESD"). If there is not sufficient space to document all, an Addendum to the ESD may be drafted. The seller's agent is required to complete the Agent Visual Inspection Disclosure (C.A.R. Form AVID). Any documentation in the seller's or seller's agent's possession that is likely to affect the buyer's interest level or offer price must be provided to the buyer's agent for buyer review. This includes any inspection reports received, substandard violation notices, tax documentation showing large special assessments, easements on the property, estimates, or invoices related to the property.

Upon submitting this disclosure package to the buyer's agent, you should request written confirmation that the buyer has reviewed the package and is still interested in proceeding with the transaction. This disclosure package must be provided to all buyers upon receipt of their offer to ensure that time is not wasted on buyers who are not serious.

Selecting Offers

The most competitive offers are generally financed offers. Owner-occupants submit financed offers, and they are emotional buyers, often willing to offer whatever it takes to win the offer bidding process. Financed offers include FHA and conventional loans. However, these buyers will request a price reduction if the property doesn't appraise at the purchase price value unless the seller requests to have the appraisal contingency removed.

Conventional loans are preferred over FHA loans because they result in fewer lender-required repairs and generally close sooner and with fewer difficulties. If proceeding with an FHA offer, a seller may request the buyer to pay for all lender-required repairs, using the seller's choice of vendor, and if the buyer is motivated to purchase the property, they will agree to these types of terms.

With an FHA loan, the appraisal serves two purposes: determining the property's market value and whether the home meets the General Acceptability Criteria established by the U.S. Department of Housing and Urban Development (HUD).

Examples of lender-required repairs for both conventional and FHA loans include the local and state law requirements for retrofitting: items such as smoke and carbon monoxide detectors installed and operating, and water heater bracing.

FHA property condition requirements are more stringent. Some examples of what an FHA appraiser looks for include: that the roof is in good condition, no presence of lead-based paint (peeling paint), the heating source must be safe and functional, there must be an operating stove, and that there are no illegal improvements made. Examples of illegal improvements include a converted garage or restroom that is not built to state or local codes or built without permits. The loan approval process will be delayed until all lender required repairs have been made and the appraiser reinspects the proper to sign off.

Generally, cash offers are the most desirable to accept if their offer price is amongst the highest because they can close the quickest with no complications, especially if the offer has no contingencies.

Countering Offers

The next step is to issue a seller's counter, reject any of the terms proposed by the buyer, and propose additional terms to protect the seller. You should not ask the seller how they wish to proceed. You should make a recommendation as to which terms to counter and why. Your seller should then let you know how they want to proceed.

The buyer is then able to either accept your counter offer, counter with a buyer's counter, or choose not to accept your counter offer. In some circumstances, the buyer and seller will negotiate through multiple counters as part of the negotiation process. This negotiation usually determines who will pay for closing related expenses, which vendors will be used throughout the escrow process and the deadlines for the buyer's removal of contingencies.

When to Use a Counter and When to Use an Addendum

A **Counter** is a statement or action made to refute, oppose, or nullify another statement or action. The definition of an **Addendum** is a thing to be added, an addition.

Therefore, if a buyer's agent puts in an offer, and a few days later buyer wants to modify the offer, the buyer's agent should issue an addendum. If the buyer's agent wants to make an additional modification to the offer later, again, an additional addendum should be issued.

If you respond to the offer with a counter, the buyer's agent should reply with a counter, not an addendum.

Assembling the Contract Package

To create the complete contract package, you should compile all necessary documents as outlined below. Remember to cut out cover pages and other unnecessary/outdated pages.

It is vital to carefully verify that all signatures, initials, spellings, and information are correct and present where necessary. The pre-approval letter must reflect the correct purchase price and type of financing, and the proof of funds must be current, dated within the past 30 days, and liquid.

Typically the contract package will include the following:

- State Purchase Contract
- Addenda
- Counters
- Disclosures – you should verify with the State's Association of Realtors to confirm which disclosures are required in your state and for the type of transaction being handled (Probate/ Trust/Bankruptcy, REO/Foreclosure, Res 1-4 units, Res 5+ units, Commercial & Industrial/Vacant Land, Mobile Home, etc.).
    - Disclosure Regarding Real Estate Agency Relationship (C.A.R. Form AD): a disclosure of the types of agency relationships possible in a real estate transaction, not a disclosure of the actual agency relationship applicable to the particular transaction.
    - Natural Hazard Disclosure (NHD Report) – The NHD form covers six natural hazard zone disclosures (Earthquake Fault Zone, Seismic Hazard Zone, State Fire Responsibility Area, Very High Fire Hazard Severity Zone, Flood Zone A, and Inundation Zones. The seller has an obligation to disclose if the property is in any of those zones. Third-party reporting companies are most often used to make these necessary disclosures.
    - Agent Visual Inspection Disclosure (C.A.R. Form AVID)
    - Exempt Seller Disclosure (C.A.R. Form ESD)
    - Water Heater and Smoke Detector Compliance (C.A.R. Form WHSD)
    - Seller's Affidavit of Nonforeign Status and/or California Withholding Exemption (C.A.R. Form AS) - can be used to demonstrate the seller is exempt from the Federal or state withholding laws or both.
    - Lead-Based Paint and Lead-Based Paint Hazards Disclosure, Acknowledgement and Addendum (C.A.R. Form FLD)
- Pre-Approval Letter – must include the buyer's name, dated in the past 30 days, and specify the type of financing being obtained and whether the buyer is an owner occupant or an investor.
- Proof of Funds – in the form of a bank letter or bank account statements. Must include buyer's name, dated in the past 30 days, include all pages, and funds must be liquid or explain the length of time it will take to become liquid.

Receiving, Reviewing, and Executing the Contract Package

After the contract package has been fully assembled and all documents have been signed and initialed by all parties, you should submit the contract package to your seller for execution.

Sending the Fully Executed Contract to the Buyer's Agent

The buyer's closing period begins when they receive the fully executed contract. If you do not send the fully executed contract to the buyer's agent right away, delays to closing can be blamed on you. You should strive to do all you can to maintain excellent performance and reputation as an agent.

Chapter 9 – Managing the Escrow Process

Chapter Overview

Chapter 9 looks at the numerous activities that should occur from the time an escrow company is notified to open escrow and assigns an escrow number to the time when the keys are turned in to the buyer and money to the seller (and you get paid, of course!).

The escrow process is divided into five phases. The first phase includes activities to perform just before opening escrow, followed by initial escrow period activities, activities throughout escrow, activities during the final part of escrow, and activities immediately once escrow closes.

The chapter then looks at possible complications that may arise during the escrow process. It concludes with a survey of various residential and commercial inspections that can be performed during escrow.

Chapter Outline

The Escrow Process

Pre-Escrow Period Activities (Phase 1)

Initial Escrow Period Activities (Phase 2)

Intermediate Escrow Period Activities (Phase 3)

Activities at End of Escrow Period (Phase 4)

Pending to Sold Activities (Phase 5)

Possible Complications During the Escrow Period

Residential Inspections

Commercial Inspections

The Escrow Process

In California (and some other states), the escrow process requires hiring a neutral third party, an escrow agent, who will hold the buyer's funds to meet the terms and conditions of a written purchase contract between a buyer and a seller.

The following steps will help create a smooth and efficient escrow process, allowing for the transfer of real property between the seller and the buyer (see Figure 31). The steps are categorized into five phases. You will handle these steps.

You should email your seller at least once a week to update them on the closing status and one week before the closing date.

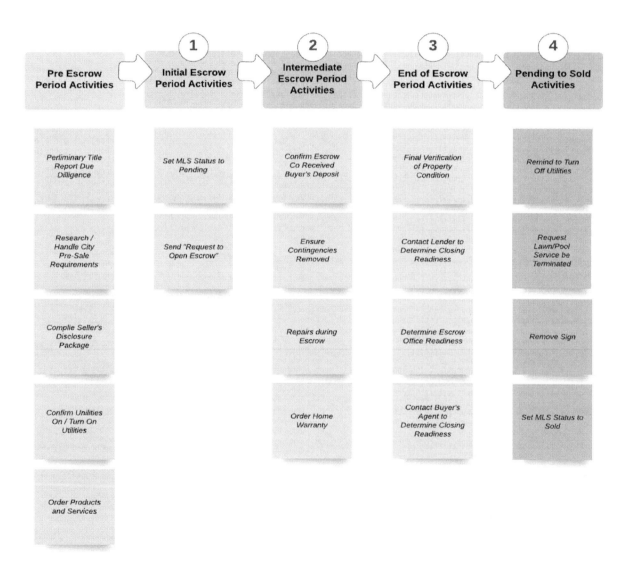

Figure 31 - The Escrow Process

Pre Escrow Period Activities (Phase 1):

- Preliminary title report due diligence
- Research and handle city pre-sale requirements
- Compile seller's disclosure package
- Confirm utilities on/turn on utilities
- Order products and services

Initial Escrow Period Activities (Phase 2):

- Set MLS status to Pending
- Send "Request to Open Escrow" email

Intermediate Escrow Period Activities (Phase 3):

- Confirm that escrow received buyer's deposit
- Ensure contingencies are removed
- Repairs required to be made during escrow
- Order home warranty plan

Activities at End of Escrow Period (Phase 4):

These are typically handled one week prior to closing.

- Contact lender to determine closing readiness
- Determine escrow office readiness
- Contact buyer's agent to determine closing readiness
- Final verification of property condition

Pending to Sold Activities (Phase 5)

- Reminder to turn off utilities
- Request lawn/pool services be terminated
- Remove sign
- Set MLS status to Sold

Pre-Escrow Period Activities (Phase 1):

Preliminary Title Report Due Diligence

The preliminary title report is a report prepared before issuing a policy of title insurance that identifies ownership of a property and any title defects, liens, restrictions, easements, and encumbrances that will not be covered under a subsequent title insurance policy.

It is customary for a real estate agent to order the preliminary title report once there's a fully ratified contract and escrow is opened. However, it is better to order it as soon as a listing agreement is signed to handle any title matters immediately and prevent delays during escrow. You should request that the title and escrow officers review the report and provide their feedback, advising on any title issues and any documentation required to address vesting, the chain of title, and liens.

Liens can be from a mortgage company, city department, utility company, or contractors. The title company will request proof showing these liens have been paid off, or, if they haven't been paid off, they may request a payoff demand from the entity who placed a lien so that it can be paid through escrow. In other situations, if a lien is placed by individuals who are no longer living, and there is no proof that it's been paid in full, the seller may have the option to indemnify the buyer for that lien.

The documentation requested should be submitted to the title and escrow officers as soon as possible so that escrow is a smooth and expedient process, once there's a fully ratified contract in place.

Research and Handle City Pre-Sale Requirements

Some cities have real property pre-sale requirements. Other cities don't have pre-sale requirements. These are requirements that must be met before the close of escrow. It's customary for a real estate agent to address these requirements once escrow is opened. It is better to conduct your due diligence to identify the city's pre-sale requirements as soon as a listing agreement is signed.

Some cities require an inspection of the property, some are exterior only, and others require interior inspections. Other cities require only a permit report to be issued, and others require a system-generated report that shows liens that may have been placed by the local safety agencies, such as the fire department.

To prevent delays in escrow and disclose the results of the inspection or report that is issued by the city, it is essential that you call the city where the property is located and inquire what the pre-sale requirements are, which refers to any requirements that must be met before a change in property ownership.

You will be required to complete an application and submit it to the city, which has a turnaround time for responding to the application. It may take 7-14 days for an inspector to visit the property for an inspection and an additional number of days to generate the inspection report. For those cities that don't require an inspection and instead only conduct a search of their database(s) and generate a report, there's also a turnaround time to receiving the report. Therefore, it is important to ensure that you identify the city pre-sale requirements as soon as possible once the listing agreement has been signed.

Compile the Disclosure Package

The disclosure package is a collection of documents, reports, inspections, and questionnaires that the seller prepares for potential buyers. The seller discloses everything they know about the property and anything that would materially affect a buyer's decision to purchase. The buyer's agent and the buyer should review the disclosure package before writing an offer on a property.

Disclosures are documents that relay important information to the buyer at the beginning of the closing transaction. Per the Purchase Agreement, these disclosures must be delivered to the buyer during the inspection period to ensure that all known facts about the property are revealed. It is best to issue the disclosure package to all buyers before the buyer submitting an offer. This includes any city pre-sale requirements such as city reports.

The information disclosed in these disclosures may impact the buyer's decision on a purchase price. The disclosures must be signed by the buyer and returned to you before offer acceptance.

If the property was previously in escrow, you should request the inspection report obtained by the prior buyer's agent and include it as part of the disclosure package. You should also disclose any known information about the property that the agent may have been told by neighbors, or the previous buyer's agent, for example.

State Required Disclosures

After your seller completes and signs the disclosures legally required by C.A.R., you email them to the buyer's agent for the agent's and buyer's review and signature. This includes disclosures such as the C.A.R. Agent Visual Inspection Disclosure (AVID), which provides an opportunity for you to disclose any visible items and/or condition of the property as a result of a visual inspection. It is good to include photos of the items being disclosed within the AVID form. Per the Purchase Agreement, the property must be delivered in the same condition as it was at the time of acceptance. Therefore it's best to document pre-existing conditions, so they are not claimed as new conditions during the escrow process. The buyer's agent is also required to conduct a visual inspection and issue an AVID for buyer and seller signatures.

Refer to section "Assemble the Contract Package" in Chapter 8 for an explanation of the other legally required disclosures.

The buyer's agent must return the ratified disclosures to you to store and record receipt. You should review the disclosures to ensure they have been signed, dated, and initialed correctly. If anything is missing, you should alert the buyer's agent to complete the disclosure(s) correctly and resubmit.

It is best to prepare the seller's disclosure package and have the seller sign along with the listing agreement. The Purchase Agreement specifies that the seller must provide all disclosures and reports to the buyer within seven days of offer acceptance – that is the default. It is best to provide the buyer's agent with disclosures and reports before buyers submit an offer. They are signed by the buyer and buyer's agent and returned to the listing agent with their offer. This practice ensures a disclosure item is not used as a reason to cancel the transaction or for buyers to lower their purchase price.

Confirm Utilities On / Turn On Utilities

You should confirm that all utilities are on before beginning the escrow process to prevent any delays. If financing is being obtained, the appraiser may test appliances to ensure they are in working order. If utilities are not on, the inspection will fail, and the appraiser would issue a condition to have utilities turned on and require a reinspection. This would incur additional costs to the buyer. Besides, utilities must be on for the home inspections. Per the Purchase Agreement, the seller must have the utilities on throughout the escrow process.

If the seller cannot have utilities turned on, this term should be negotiated out before you enter escrow during the offer negotiations process. For example, it is unsafe to turn on utilities when there are exposed electrical wires and if there are water leaks.

When turning on the water, it's essential to have someone at the property in case the faucets have been previously turned to the on position, or, in case there is a leak, to prevent flooding of the property.

Order Products and Services

Products such as the NHD (Natural Hazard Disclosure) report are usually ordered once escrow has opened. However, it is best to order them immediately. For example, suppose there is limited access to the property because it is occupied. In that case, it may be beneficial for the seller to pay for the inspections and have you order them once the listing agreement has been signed so that they can be included in the disclosure package and buyers can review them before writing an offer. If inspection reports are provided to buyers before writing their offers, it is reasonable for the seller to request offers that have the inspection contingency waived.

NHD (Natural Hazard Disclosure)

Many of the required hazard disclosures are included in the "Natural Hazard Disclosures" (NHD) report available for purchase through third-party providers.

It is legally required in California that the seller provide disclosures related to the hazards, and it is customary for the seller to pay for the NHD report.

Regardless of who will be paying for it, it is best to request the escrow officer to order it as soon as possible, once the listing assignment has been signed so that it can be included in the seller's disclosure package.

Sellers and agents are required to review and sign the NHD receipt, and it should be included with the seller's disclosure package and provided to all interested buyers before offer acceptance.

The NHD specifies potential environmental hazards associated with the property, such as whether it's at risk for fires or earthquakes and whether it's in a flood zone.

The third-party NHD provider will deliver the NHD via email to you, and you will forward it to you your seller for their records. You will include the NHD receipt in the seller's disclosure package for your seller's review and signature. You will first sign and date the NHD receipt as the seller's agent. Once the seller returns the seller's disclosure package to you, it will be provided to the buyer's agents along with the full NHD report to provide to interested buyers for review prior to submitting their offers.

Termite Inspection Report

Buyers may request in the Purchase Agreement that a termite inspection report is provided to buyers, to be paid either by your seller or the buyer and usually indicate that it is the seller's choice of a vendor that must be used. If this is the case, you should inform the buyer's agent as soon as possible which vendor will be used.

You should schedule the termite inspection with the vendor and provide the property's lockbox code and billing instructions. It is customary that the vendor is paid through closing on the settlement statement.

The vendor will deliver the Termite Inspection Report via email to you. You should forward the Termite Inspection Report to your seller for your review and to the buyer's agent and escrow officer upon receipt. The invoice should also be emailed to the escrow officer by you to ensure the vendor is paid once escrow closes.

Initial Escrow Period Activities (Phase 2)

This phase begins once a fully executed contract has been procured. This is the start of the escrow process. Once the escrow process has started, several steps must be taken to ensure that the property is ready to be sold. By completing these tasks, you help to ensure a smooth transaction.

Set MLS Status to Pending

Once you receive the ratified purchase contract, you must communicate this in the MLS to the agent community within 24 hours by setting the MLS status to "Pending".

Suppose your seller wishes to continue and receive offers for the property while in escrow and accept another buyer's offer as a backup offer. In that case, you should set the property to Active Under Contract status (or equivalent) on the MLS. Accepting another offer in the backup position will put pressure on the buyer currently in escrow to perform. If the current buyer doesn't perform and that contract and escrow are canceled, you will be able to open escrow with the buyer in the backup position.

Send "Request to Open Escrow" Email

You should take a leadership role in facilitating the escrow process. Most agents do not do this, but you will be an excellent agent! On the day that the fully executed contract is received, you should prepare an email and send it to the buyer's agent and the escrow officer. The email includes all parties' contact information and a summary of contract terms. The fully executed contract should be included as an attachment.

The "Request to Open Escrow" email summarizes key terms agreed to in the purchase agreement and includes the following:

- Introduction of the listing agent, buyer's agent, loan officer, and escrow officer, along with their contact information.
- Confirmation of products ordered by the listing agent.
- Request for escrow officer to provide the wire instructions for the earnest money deposit (EMD) and opening package.

- Instructions to buyer's agent on next steps, which may include: ensuring buyer deposits the EMD to escrow, a reminder to order inspections, confirmation of the costs and items that seller and buyer have agreed to pay as per contract, and request to order any necessary products, such as the home warranty plan.
- Reminder to the loan officer to order the appraisal.
- Report the utilities status, are gas, electricity, and water on? It is critical to confirm the utilities status since this impacts the home and appraisal inspections, if applicable. If utilities are off, the home inspector and appraiser will need to re-inspect the property once utilities are on, and a re-inspection fee will apply.
- HOA information. Confirm whether the property has a Homeowner's Association and, if so, include their contact information.
- Contingency removal due dates for loan, appraisal, title, inspection.

You should consider sending a copy of this email separately to your seller for information purposes and as self-promotion.

Intermediate Escrow Period Activities (Phase 3)

The closing tasks in this third phase are some of the most important tasks you will handle in the closing process. Completion of these tasks may allow the transaction to come to full fruition. During this phase, the buyer may or may not decide to continue with the purchase of the property if there are contingencies.

Confirm that Escrow Received Buyer's Deposit

Most purchase agreements specify that the buyer's earnest money deposit (EMD) is due in escrow within 24 hours of offer acceptance.

The earnest money deposit essentially serves as motivation for the buyer to close the transaction. The buyer runs the risk of losing this deposit if the buyer chooses to cancel the transaction after removing contingencies. Also, suppose the transaction is not completed by the closing date. In that case, the buyer runs the risk of losing the earnest money deposit to the seller if the seller chooses not to extend the closing date, and the buyer is unable to close on time.

Because the EMD is a vital asset in guaranteeing the close of the sale, you need to ensure that the money is delivered to escrow within the time specified in the contract. Otherwise, the buyer can drag the escrow process. Some agents issue a Notice to Buyer to Perform upon offer acceptance, enforcing the buyer's contractual obligation to deliver the deposit per terms of the contract.

You should send an email to the escrow officer to follow up on the status of the deposit on the day that it is due. If the deposit has not been received, you should request an update from the buyer's agent.

Ensure Contingencies Are Removed

The contingency period is the time allowed by the purchase agreement for the buyer to obtain loan approval, complete inspections, obtain an appraisal, review and approve the preliminary title report, and satisfy any other contingencies to which the purchase is subject. The purchase contract is contingent upon the fulfillment of certain conditions.

According to the terms of the purchase agreement, if any contingencies are not fulfilled, the buyer can cancel the contract and escrow and have the buyer's earnest money deposit returned. Time periods for each contingency or contractual obligation are stated in the contract.

The Statute of Frauds requires real estate contracts to be in writing to be enforceable. Therefore any amendment to the contract in terms of removal of contingencies, including altering the time during which either must be accomplished, must also be in writing. C.A.R. form Contingency Removal (CR) may be used. The seller often requires contingencies to be removed before proceeding with repairs, providing an incentive for buyers to remove them early or on time.

You should monitor the closing process to ensure a timely closing and the terms of the purchase contract are being met and that the buyer performs as per the contract.

The buyer's agent helps the buyer remove contingencies by completing the contingency removal form (C.A.R. form CR) that specifies that the buyer is satisfied, wants to proceed with the transaction, and gives up the right to the EMD. The buyer signs this form.

Should the buyer request to cancel the transaction after all contingencies have been removed, the right to the deposit will have already been surrendered.

Two days before a contingency removal is due, you should send an email reminder to the buyer's agent requesting the removal of the contingency. It is a good idea to issue a Notice to Buyer to Perform (C.A.R. Form NBP) to the buyer two days before a contingency removal being due, to enforce the buyer's contractual obligation to remove contingencies on time. Suppose the buyer doesn't perform and remove contingencies two days after the NBP has been issued. In that case, the seller can proceed with issuing a Cancellation of Contract, Release of Deposit, and Cancellation of Escrow (C.A.R. form CC) and cancel both the contract and escrow using this form.

Request for Repairs

The buyer's agent may send a Request for Repairs form to you, requesting either a credit or repairs to be made due to an inspection completed on the property. The buyer's agent will include the inspection report and may include bids. These buyer requests can be made even if the terms of the contract specify an "A-Is" sale.

No repairs may be completed without the seller's written authorization.

It is a good idea to avoid these types of requests by scheduling a call or virtually meeting with the buyer and buyer's agent before offering acceptance and setting the proper expectations, letting the buyer know the seller will not be making any repairs nor issuing credits, and that the seller will merely move on to the next buyer if the request is made.

Obtain Bids

Your seller may immediately indicate that the property is being sold in "As Is" condition and reject the request, or request that the bids are presented once they are ready.

Your seller will decide how much of a credit to issue. Sellers typically prefer to issue a credit to limit liability and save time, and in most cases, will only make repairs if they are lender-required.

Suppose the financing type obtained by the buyer is FHA. In that case, you should include the appraisal along with the Request for Repairs and bids for review since the lender-required repairs are listed as "Subject to:" items in the FHA appraisal, and include photos and details on the repairs being requested.

You should obtain the bids from the seller's choice of vendor. The seller's choice of vendor for any repairs should be included as a term in the offer negotiations process. Although the buyer's agent may issue the Request for Repair form, the bids should be submitted by vendors approved by the seller to ensure that the vendors are qualified and are adequately insured to complete the work.

Price Reduction

Depending on the extent of repairs, a request to complete the repairs can delay the closing process. The buyer may opt to request a price reduction instead of the completion of repairs.

You can either approve, counter, or reject the request for a price reduction.

A price reduction may not always be related to repairs, either. Depending on the type of financing, a price reduction may be necessary to obtain the loan if the property does not appraise at the purchase price. It is a good idea to require that the buyer remove the appraisal contingency before offering acceptance to reduce the chance of a price reduction request. By removing the appraisal contingency, the buyer must pay the difference between the appraised value and the purchase price.

The lender will order an appraisal for the property to determine the value of the property. The appraisal report will identify any lender-required repairs as well as the value of the property.

Request for Credit

Similarly to requesting a price reduction, the buyer may request credit instead of repairs as it causes fewer closing delays. A Request for Credit differs from a Request for a Price reduction as it does not change the value of the buyer's purchase price.

A credit awarded by the seller to the buyer through closing will be added to the settlement statement. The credit will be noted as an expense to the seller rather than any change in the purchase price. Because of this, the value of the property remains the same.

Repairs During Escrow

Repairs, including termite repairs, should be completed by vendors who are properly licensed and insured. The seller is required to provide the buyer with receipts of work completed.

If the buyer or the seller has agreed to pay for repairs, You will notify the approved vendor to complete the work.

If the buyer is obtaining FHA financing, the appraiser will need to reinspect the property after all repairs have been made. Therefore, all utilities that have been turned off during repairs must be turned back on immediately after repairs have been completed to avoid any delay to closing.

Termite Repairs

The termite report will indicate if repairs are needed and describe items as either Section 1 or Section 2. Section 1 items are those items that exist today in the dwelling – actual evidence of wood-destroying pests: termite, dry rot, or fungus. If a termite inspection is completed, lenders require that Section 1 repairs are made before the close of escrow.

Section 2 items are those that, if left untreated or not repaired, can become Section 1 items. These are areas where wood-destroying pests can flourish or elements can cause wood damage. For example, a pile of wood logs, or a home with wood siding with a sprinkler system and one of the sprinklers hits the side of the house and begins to warp the wood, and therefore, it has the potential of turning into a Section 1 item. Lenders don't require Section 2 repairs to be made during escrow. However, buyers should note them and make the necessary repairs after the close of escrow to prevent them from becoming problems in the future.

Suppose the buyer has requested a termite inspection on the Purchase Agreement. In that case, the lender will require that the termite repairs are completed and Section 1 Clearance provided by the termite company on the property before close. Section 1 Clearance is a certification issued by the licensed termite company when all Section 1 termite repairs have been remedied, including fumigation, replacing damaged wood, and/or chemical treatment.

If the termite repairs are to be completed, you will order the work to be completed by the termite company. Most of the time, the termite company will have specific guidelines that you must adhere to regarding the property's preparation for treatment.

It is your responsibility to call the gas company, turn off the gas before the start of work, and request the gas to be turned back immediately after it has been completed.

It is essential to advise the buyer's agent of the repair schedule, so they do not schedule any inspections or appraisals during this time.

In transactions where repairs are required, and the offers have contingencies, it is good to have the buyer remove all contingencies before repairs are completed. The types of repairs include termite repairs or lender required repairs on FHA transactions. Completing these repairs after the removal of all contingencies allows the seller to collect the buyer's deposit and, in turn, pay for these repairs if the buyer chooses to cancel the transaction.

Retrofitting

When there's a transfer of real property ownership, California and most cities and counties require compliance with specific health and safety, and water conservation requirements. First and foremost, state requirements must be met (if there are any). Depending on where the property is located, county or city requirements must be adhered to. For properties located within a city's limits, that city's requirements must be met. If the property is located in an unincorporated area outside of a city's limits, the county's requirements must be adhered to.

You should have a vendor specializing in retrofitting compliance services conduct a retrofitting inspection and provide a bid for the work required to be in compliance. The work should be completed before the close of escrow. If the property is occupied, it is prudent to conduct a retrofitting inspection and complete the work as soon as possible to prevent any liability associated with missing detectors or unstrapped water heater in case of a fire or earthquake.

In the state of California, retrofitting must be completed before the close of escrow. The State of California addresses both health and safety and water conservation requirements.

Health and Safety

Many states, including California, require that operating smoke detectors are installed in the proper locations. Single-family properties may have battery-powered detectors, and multifamily properties require hardwired detectors. California State Building Code requires that smoke alarms be located in:

- On every floor
- In each bedroom
- The hallway outside the bedrooms

California law also requires all dwelling units intended for human occupancy with fossil-burning appliances, fireplaces, or an attached garage to be retrofitted with a carbon monoxide detection device. These devices may be battery-powered or a plug-in with a battery back-up. They can be combined with a smoke detector but must also emit a distinct alarm to signal the presence of dangerous CO levels. They must be replaced every seven years.

California law requires that all water heaters be braced, anchored, or strapped to resist falling or horizontal displacement due to earthquake motion. The water heater with a tank must have two straps, one in the top 1/3 of the tank and the other on the bottom 1/3, no closer than 4" from controls. Blocking must be installed when the tank is 1-1/2" or more from the wall to prevent excessive movement.

For commercial properties, smoke detectors are required only for areas used or defined as sleeping quarters, as well as hallways that give access to sleeping rooms. Battery operated or hardwired is acceptable. Each story of the dwelling, including basements and habitable attics, requires a smoke detector. Carbon monoxide detectors are only required in buildings with fossil fuel-burning appliances, attached garages, and sleeping areas. They are required outside each separate sleeping area, the hallways, and on each story of the dwelling, including basements and habitable attics. Water heater strapping requirements apply to commercial properties as well, where there is a water heater.

Note that each city and county has its own requirements, which must be adhered to in addition to the state requirements. For example, the City of Los Angeles has the following additional requirements:

- Impact Hazard Glazing - Tempered glass or the application of impact glazing on all sliding doors
- Earthquake Gas Shut-Off Valves - Buildings containing fuel gas piping require an Earthquake Gas Shut Off Valve and also require a permit
- Egress - Every sleeping room below the fourth story shall have at least one opearable window or door approved for emergency escape or rescue that shall open directly into a public street, public alley, yard, or exit court
- Security Lighting and Locks - All apartment buildings (those containing three or more dwelling units) shall be provided with security lighting and locks. Exterior lighting shall be provided in parking areas, walkways, recreation areas, and similar locations and at each dwelling unit's entrance. Interior lighting shall be provided in recreation or service rooms and parking garages. Locks shall be provided at all doors and windows leading into each dwelling unit.

Water Conservation

California law defines the water conservation requirements as follows: ultra low flow toilets not to exceed 1.6 gallons per flush, showerheads not to exceed 2.5 gallons per minute, and faucet flow restriction (aerators) not to exceed 2.2 gallons per minute. The seller can either make improvements to adhere to these requirements or just disclose the status of the fixtures to the buyer.

Note that each city has its requirements related to water conservation. For example, in the City of Los Angeles, the LADWP (Los Angeles Department of Water and Power) requires improvements to be made, if needed, to adhere to Municipal Water Conservation Ordinance and requires a seller to submit a Certificate of Compliance, certifying that the property is in compliance, prior to the close of escrow. Note that it is possible to obtain a Waiver from the LADWP and delay making these improvements if the property is uninhabitable and the buyer plans on renovating the property after the close of escrow.

Order Home Warranty Plan

A home warranty plan is usually a one-year service contract protecting a home buyer from the cost of unexpected repairs or replacements of appliances and major home systems.

Some buyers request in their offer that a home warranty plan is ordered, to be paid for either by the buyer or the seller. Usually, the request is to utilize the buyer's choice of vendor.

If the buyer's choice of vendor has been agreed to in the Purchase Agreement, you should email the buyer's agent and requests that the buyer's agent order the home warranty plan. You should also remind the buyer's agent who is paying for the warranty and that it will be paid through escrow on the settlement statement.

If it is the seller's choice of vendor, you should order the warranty through either your seller or your preferred provider. The request to purchase is made via email, specifying the not to exceed dollar amount and type of coverage required with the buyer's name, property address, and buyer's agent's contact information and billing instructions. This should be handled towards the end of escrow. Once all contingencies have been removed.

Activities at End of Escrow Period (Phase 4)

After all lender conditions and requirements have been met, the lender must prepare for closing. You are responsible for coordinating with the buyer's agent and the escrow office for the loan documents to be signed by the buyer.

The lender can delay the closing by requesting an extension.

Once loan documents have been signed, and funding is completed, the escrow officer will set up the file to record. It is possible to have recordings completed on the same day as funding in some counties such as San Bernardino. In some counties such as Los Angeles, recordings are only available on the following day.

You should take the lead and communicate with the lender, escrow, and buyer's agent to ensure progress is being made.

Final Verification of Property Condition

Once the buyer's inspection contingency period expires, the buyer has no right to enter the seller's property until the final verification of property condition. The buyer has the right to a final walkthrough of the property to confirm that the property is in the same condition as it was when the buyer's offer was accepted and that any repairs that were required to be made have been completed, and that seller has complied with the terms of the contract. If the property is not in the same condition or repairs were not made, they can be addressed immediately before the close of escrow, and the buyer may exercise their legal rights. A buyer should sign off on the Verification of Property Condition (C.A.R. Form VP) once the final walkthrough has been completed and before the close of escrow. It is customary that this is completed once loan documents have been signed prior to funding. The VP form is used to document the buyer's findings or the buyer's inspector at the time of the final verification. If the buyer doesn't wish to conduct a final verification inspection, the buyer should check off the box on the VP form, indicating that the buyer waives their right to do so.

Contact Lender to Determine Closing Readiness

You should email and call the lender contact one week prior to the closing date to determine whether closing will occur on time. You must determine if the lender is ready to have buyers sign loan documents.

Typically, if the buyer is signing at least one week before the closing date, the transaction will likely close on time. Any later and there may be delays.

You should report the lender's status to your seller. If it is determined that the closing will be delayed, you should work with the buyer's agent to arrive at a reasonable new closing date.

The buyer's agent will send an Extension of Time Addendum to you to be sent to your seller for review and signature. If the extension is granted, a per diem may be charged to the buyer, depending on the Purchase Agreement's terms. It a good idea to include a per diem charge to the buyer for any delays caused by the buyer. This provides added motivation for the buyer to perform in a timely manner.

Determine Escrow Office Readiness

You should email and call the closing office one week prior to closing to request a copy of the estimated closing statement for review and determine if the escrow officer is missing anything from you or the buyer's agent.

You should also confirm information obtained from the lender, such as when the buyers are signing loan documents and the funding and recording dates. If there are any issues, the escrow officer should advise what might prevent recording on the scheduled date.

You should review the estimated settlement statement to ensure that all products and services that must be paid through closing have been accounted for and are being paid for by the appropriate party. If any are missing, you should provide those invoices to the escrow officer to be included for payment.

Contact Buyer's Agent to Determine Closing Readiness

You should email and call the buyer's agent one week prior to closing to confirm the closing date and the information provided by the lender and escrow officer, such as when the buyers are signing loan documents and the funding and recording dates.

If there is a discrepancy in this information, update the other parties and proceed with an Extension of Time Addendum if the closing date will be delayed.

Pending to Sold Activities (Phase 5)

Once you receive confirmation of recording from the escrow office, tasks need to be performed to ensure that the property is prepared to be transferred to the buyer.

Reminder to Turn Off Utilities

You should remind your seller to turn off utilities a few days before closing (loan funding is a good marker for this).

Request Lawn/Pool Services Be Terminated

Before a property closing, you should notify the vendor(s) providing yard and/or pool maintenance of the closing date and to confirm the final service date. You should remind the vendor that photos from the date of final services should be emailed to you.

Remove Sign

You should contact your sign installation company to go out to the property asap and remove the sign and post.

Set MLS Status to Sold

You should set the MLS status to sold. As part of the process, you typically have to indicate, at a minimum, the sale date, sale price, and the buyer's agent name.

Possible Complications During the Escrow Period

You should email the buyer's agent and the lender throughout the closing process to ensure the closing is timely. If there is a delay, an Extension of Time Addendum must be completed by the buyer's agent and signed by the buyer.

The Addendum should be provided to you at least one week prior to the closing date or as soon as you identify a delay.

If the buyer causes a delay in closing, you may charge the buyer a per diem fee. The per diem fee varies anywhere from $50 to $200 per day. If the lender causes the delay, it's considered to be a delay caused by the buyer, as the lender is a vendor selected by the buyer.

The amount to be charged is typically addressed in the contract. Some sellers may choose not to charge a per diem fee, even if the delays are at the buyer's fault.

The buyer's agent may request to have the per diem fee waived if the delay was caused by the escrow company or other circumstances not related to the buyer. Possible complications are discussed in the following sections (see Figure 32).

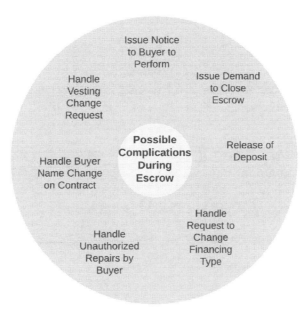

Figure 32 - Possible Complications During Escrow

Issue a Notice to Buyer to Perform

Sometimes a buyer doesn't do what the buyer promised to do, for example, making a deposit or removing any of the contingencies. Common law in California allows one party to cancel if the other party has committed a material breach. The RPA has created a contractual right to cancel but only after the seller has delivered to the buyer a Notice to Buyer to Perform (C.A.R. form NBP).

Suppose the buyer does not remove contingencies the day they are due. In that case, you should prepare a notice to the buyer, indicating that if the buyer does not perform and remove contingencies as indicated in the contract within 48 hours of receipt (or period specified in the contract), the seller will cancel the transaction.

You should prepare the Notice to Buyer to Perform (C.A.R. form NBP) and forward it to your seller for signature. Once the seller signs it, you forward it to the buyer's agent to be signed by the buyer. The 48 hour period (or until the previously agreed time as per contract, whichever occurs last) begins once the NBP is issued to the buyer. By delivering the NBP, there is a document establishing that no more time or delay will be allowed and that the seller is reasserting the need to comply with the contract terms.

Issue Demand to Close Transaction

If the buyer's agent is not responsive to emails or phone calls, and by the 3rd day before closing, an update has not been provided, you should prepare the Demand to Close Escrow (C.A.R. form DCE) and send it to your seller for signature. The seller signed DCE would then be delivered to the buyer's agent for the buyer's signature. In this case, the Notice to Buyer to Perform (NBP) would not be used since the seller must return a buyer's deposit after canceling following the issuance of an NBP, but there is no such obligation to do so following the issuance of a DCE.

The buyer who has already removed all contingencies is more than likely to be in breach of contract for failure to close and may not have a legal right to have the deposit returned. This form puts the receiving party on notice that escrow must be closed in three days (or other specified time) or risk cancellation. C.A.R. form CC can be used to cancel the contract once that time expires.

The Statute of Frauds requires real estate contracts to be in writing to be enforceable. Therefore, it requires that any amendment to the contract in terms of cancellation must also be in writing using the C.A.R. form Cancellation of Contract, Release of Deposit and Joint Escrow Instructions (C.A.R. form CC). Verbal cancellation is not enforceable.

Disagreement on Release of Deposit

Both parties, buyer and seller, must sign a cancellation of escrow included in section 2 of the C.A.R. form CC. Sometimes buyer and seller may disagree on who is entitled to the deposit money, and sometimes one of the parties refuses to sign escrow instructions releasing the deposit. Sometimes it's not for any apparent reason but rather to make it difficult for the other party. Inaction by one forces the other party to take legal action or enter into mediation to avoid the time and expense of pursuing legal action. Sometimes a party has disappeared or is unresponsive, and it's impossible to get that party to sign. Using the C.A.R. form Seller Demand for Release of Deposit or Buyer Demand for Release of Deposit (C.A.R. form SDRD or BDRD), one party makes a demand for the deposit. If the other doesn't object in 10 days, escrow has the authority to release the deposit to the party making the demand. If an objection is made, then escrow will continue to hold the funds until a mutual instruction is made.

Handle Request to Change Financing Type

During the escrow period, the buyer may require to change the loan's financing type. This change in contract terms requires an addendum to be prepared by the buyer's agent and submitted to the seller for approval. Depending on the type of financing being obtained, your seller may choose to approve the change or cancel the transaction as the contract terms are being modified.

Handle Unauthorized Repairs by Buyer or Buyer's agent

The buyer or buyer's agent may decide to conduct repairs on the property without your authorization. When this happens, it is vital to communicate to the buyer or buyer's agent that any damages, claims, or further liabilities will be their responsibility.

The seller may also record a Notice of Non-Responsibility (C.A.R. Form NNR) to help protect the seller's interest for buyer investigations and work done on the Property at the buyer's discretion.

Handle Changes in Buyers' Names on Contracts

If the buyer's agent advises that the buyer(s) name(s) on the contract require modification, an addendum should be submitted to change the name. The addendum must be signed by the buyer and seller and submitted to the escrow officer.

Handle Vesting Change Requests

The buyer has an option on how to take title in the real property that is being purchased. The buyer may choose to consult with a real estate attorney to determine the best way to vest title. The manner of vesting will later determine ownership of the property when a party of the vesting passes away and will determine if a probate is needed or not.

When a buyer chooses to change the vesting name on title, a request must be made to the seller on an addendum, indicating the proper vesting.

Residential Inspections

To satisfy the inspection contingency, the buyer typically orders an inspection company to inspect the property and provide its report.

General Inspection

The general home inspection will identify potential issues such as problems with the roof, foundations, or possible mold. It would recommend a more in-depth and specialized inspection for each of these areas by a specialist in each respective area. For example, a roof inspection would be conducted by a roofing contractor who is well versed in identifying the issues and the cost to repair. A structural engineer would conduct a foundation inspection.

A general home inspection typically covers:

- Interior
- Exterior
- Adjacent grounds
- Parking structure
- Electrical
- Foundation
- Heating and Air
- Plumbing
- Pool and Spa
- Roof

Specialized Inspections

In addition to a general inspection, the buyer may select to have these inspections completed:

- Geological and soil inspections for hillside properties

- Moisture / Mold Inspection
- Sewer line scope inspection
- Chimney inspection
- Foundation inspection
- Sprinkler and irrigation system inspection
- Electric magnetic field rating inspection

Commercial Inspections

Commercial inspection types vary, from visual inspection to a comprehensive inspection of a building's technical components.

Typical basic commercial building inspection services include:

- Air conditioning and ventilation systems
- Document review
- Electrical systems
- Heating systems
- Interior elements
- Life safety and fire protection
- Mechanical and electrical systems
- Opinions of probable costs
- Plumbing systems
- Roof surface areas
- Site characteristics (paving, landscaping, and utilities)
- Structural frame and building envelope
- Vertical transportation
- Recommendations

Additional services that may be available include:

- Americans with Disabilities Act (ADA) assessments
- Asbestos inspections
- Elevator inspections
- Fire safety inspections
- Indoor Air Quality (IAQ) assessments
- Lead-based paint inspections
- Phase I environmental site assessments
- Radon inspections
- Sewage and treatment systems inspections
- Wood-destroying organism inspections

Part Three – What It Takes to Succeed in Real Estate Sales

Part three looks at what it takes to be a successful real estate agent. Chapter 10 looks at the skills you should possess as an agent. Chapter 11 looks at how to choose the right brokerage to join. Chapter 12 looks at how you should market yourself, your brand, and your services as an agent once you join a brokerage.

Chapter 10 – Skill You Should Possess

Chapter Overview

Chapter 10 provides a survey of the skills real estate agents need to optimize their success. Skills can be learned, so if you feel you need to, get started learning and practicing them as soon as you finish this book.

Chapter Outline

Ethics

Self-Control

Assertiveness

Analytical Thinking

Intuition and Creativity

Persuasion

Adaptability and Flexibility

Communication

Negotiation

Project Management

Skills Beneficial for Agents

Let's take a look at the skills agents should ideally possess (see Figure 33).

Figure 33 - Skills Agents Should Possess

Ethics

Have high moral principles that would lead you to strive to do all you can for your actions to result in good for others and no harm to others.

Are you all about making money, or are you concerned with doing the right thing? Are you concerned with protecting your clients and their interests? Doing the right thing for others will, in turn, protect you in this business!

Self-Control

You should have the ability to stay calm and relaxed in difficult situations and not get upset or say something inappropriate. It would help if you exhibited patience, stress tolerance, and focus during these times.

Assertiveness

Taking control of a situation and doing what needs to be done efficiently is an important quality to look for in an agent. Being assertive is the balance between being aggressive and passive. It encourages two-way communication and exchange and the sharing of opinions and thoughts. Assertiveness promotes cooperation and positive, healthy interpersonal relationships. On the other hand, passive agents are afraid to speak up, not to appear disrespectful, not to upset someone, and just to fit in. You want to be proactive, take charge, especially throughout the escrow process.

Analytical Thinking

Are you able to look at a situation and make recommendations supported by evidence?

Consider the following example. A seller requests that a property is sold with a tenant inside since the tenant has lived at the property for many years. While the tenant is underpaying rent by a substantial amount, the seller does not wish to evict the tenant due to financial hardship.

In this example, the agent needs to discuss the situation with the seller. If the agent proceeds as the seller wishes, the property will be sold substantially undervalue to an investor. The investor will pay far less since they will calculate that they will need time and money to evict the tenant to bring the property back to profitability. The tenant will lose, and so will the seller. The only winner will be an investor that the seller does not even know.

An agent that is an analytical thinker will explain this to the seller and possibly change the seller's mind. The seller could provide relocation assistance and help the tenant find a new place, and the seller will be able to sell the unit to an owner occupant for a substantially higher price.

Intuition and Creativity

To be an effective marketer, you must possess both intuition and creativity. Creativity allows for lots of ideas, and intuition provides you with the clarity and focus to determine which marketing ideas will work best for selling your property.

Persuasion

A good persuader has well developed social skills and can tap into what people think, need, and respond to. Persuasion is about being able to match client needs with viable solutions skillfully. Persuasion skills enable you to ask many questions and stay focused on problem solving while keeping the client's needs in mind as a top priority.

Adaptability and Flexibility

An adaptable and flexible agent seeks improvement and is not focused on doing things the way they have always been done. This agent will ask more questions and research ways to accomplish the goals in different ways to reveal new insights and obtain better results.

Communication

Do you communicate clearly and effectively with those around you? Do you present your clients with your points of view? Or, do you simply follow your client's instructions?

Will you be effective at communicating with the other parties during the transaction? Or, will the buyer's agent walk all over you when they make price reductions and other demands during escrow?

A great communicator is articulate and must also be able to listen actively, which requires undivided attention to understand and resolve conflict and inspire new ideas.

The communication process consists of a sender, receiver, message, communication channel, and feedback. As a sender, your messages need to be well composed, effective, and concise. As a receiver, you need to be able to provide feedback, express your opinions, and explain them.

Negotiation

Will you sit back and pass your offers from buyers' agents that have unreasonable terms without explaining to your seller why these are unreasonable offers?

Will you pass buyer's requests during escrow for approval without pushing back?

You should be able to see the deal from both sides and make wise business decisions. A negotiation begins with a common goal, such as selling a property. Conflicting interests then arise, most often regarding the price and concessions. A compromise must then be made, meaning some desired goal must be forsaken to achieve the common goal. This involves identifying and resolving all areas of disagreement. Both parties should be willing to budge and give up something tied to their interests and arrive at a final agreement, and you should be comfortable navigating these waters.

It would help if you built a rapport with buyers' agents, engage in small talk over the phone, and get to know each other, allowing for better collaboration and will more likely allow you to reach an agreement with them and make deals happen.

Project Management

Proven management skills are very beneficial to closing real estate deals.

Will you sit back and react to requests by the buyer's agent and/or escrow, or will you take a leadership role and proactively follow up with the escrow and the buyer's agent to ensure each step of the offer and escrow management processes are handled in a timely manner?

Chapter 11 – Choosing the Right Brokerage for You

Chapter Overview

Chapter 11 looks at why selecting the right broker for you is so important. The chapter then discusses 13 key factors agents should consider when choosing a broker to join. They include fees, training, Mentoring, management support, and others.

Chapter Outline

Why is broker selection so important?

13 Key Factors in Selecting a Real Estate Brokerage

Why is Broker Selection So Important?

Once you pass your real estate salesperson's state exam and receive your license, it is time to find a broker to hang your license with.

Real estate sales and leasing is a business of relationships. Relationships with clients, lenders, relationships with fellow agents, and with many others. In most cases, an essential relation you can have when getting started is with your broker. And an experienced and caring broker can be valuable in helping you become successful.

It's important to schedule calls with multiple brokerages to see if you are a good fit for them, and they are a good fit for you. You should be interviewing each other. Most brokerages are continuously looking for agents and will be happy to speak with you.

If you have not taken your exam yet, schedule interviews anyway. You can learn about various opportunities before you get your license and be ready to join the brokerage that is right for you as soon as you receive your license.

13 Key Factors in Selecting a Real Estate Brokerage

Choosing the right brokerage is critical to your success. The 13 key factors involved in making the right decision for you (see Figure 2) are:

- Commission
- Fees
- Training
- Mentoring
- Management support
- Administrative support
- Brokerage focus area(s)
- Referrals and leads
- Internet presence
- Culture
- Brokerage size
- Facilities
- Location

Figure 34 – Key Factors involved in Choosing the Right Brokerage for you

The following is a look at each of these 13 key factors in more detail.

Commission

The vast majority of agents get paid commission only. The commission is paid once a deal is closed and the property is either sold or leased. Different brokers offer different commission splits to their agents. Commissions can be negotiated in many cases as you gain more experience in the industry.

Here in Los Angeles, for example, a typical commission is 5%. If you sell a $700,000 property, the total commission is 5% of this amount. It is usually split equally between the listing agent and the buyer's agent. If you represent one side, 2.5% is 17,500. A portion of this commission goes to your broker, so if you have a 60-40 split with your broker, you get to keep 60% of 17,500, which is $10,500. Remember that you need to pay taxes on this amount but can also deduct certain expenses as an independent contractor.

What is a reasonable commission split? The answer to that depends on the following:

- Which area of the country you live in, and what standards are there
- What level of support the broker provides
- How motivated the broker is to have you join their brokerage as an agent

The key is to understand what you will be receiving, given the split offered. The split should not be your primary consideration when selecting a brokerage to start your career.

If a broker can help get your business off the ground, they should receive a reasonable portion of the commission. Remember, 100% of nothing is nothing, so why worry about the split when getting started?

Many brokerages start new agents at a 60-40% split. In these cases, most of the overhead expenses are paid by the real estate company.

Some brokers offer 100% commission. Note that they will make you pay in other ways, with transaction fees, Errors and Omissions (E&O) insurance premiums, and desk fees, and they will probably offer you very little or no assistance.

Join the brokerage you like the most, do not focus on negotiating commission and other terms. You can and should do that later once you learn the business and start to consistently close deals.

Fees

Many brokerages charge fees. Fees may include any combination of the following:

- Transaction fees
- Desk fees
- Technology Fees
- Print fees
- Copy fees
- Insurance fees

Add up all the fees to determine your monthly, annual, and/or per-transaction costs. Ask yourself this: why should any brokerage charge you any monthly or annual fees? Are they in the business of collecting fees or in the business of helping their agents close deals to everyone's benefit?

Training

Preparing for the state exam does not prepare you for creating a successful business for yourself in the real world. Now that you have a license, you need to learn many topics, including but not limited to the following:

- Determining property values based on comparables. Creating BPO reports for clients
- Filling out real estate forms and contracts for a variety of situations
- What marketing works and what is not likely to work, and why
- Communication strategies
- Negotiation strategies

Essential questions you should find answers to:

- Who will be training you?
- What is their practical experience?
- What is their training experience?

- How long have they been in real estate?
- What is their real estate experience?
- How long have they been training?
- What is the format of the training?
- How much time do they have for you?

Ongoing training is vital for any agent, given how fast technology is changing the business, regardless of how long they have been in the industry.

If a brokerage offers classes, ask to sit on one of the classes and see if you would benefit from the experience before joining the brokerage if this is your primary selection consideration. If a brokerage claims to be providing one-on-one training, ask to experience a conversation with your trainer to be, perhaps via zoom.

Mentoring

You will likely need, as most new agents do, someone to mentor you. That person should guide you at each step of your first few deals.

Your mentor will be crucial to your success. You should schedule a virtual meeting with the person who will be your mentor before deciding to join a specific brokerage. You should determine:

- How available will they be
- What their plan is
- What their compensation is for mentoring you
- If you see yourself spending time with them and learning from them.

Good mentors should love mentoring. It should be in their personality. This should be much more than about the money. You will need to see if they have the right personality for the role and for you given your own personality.

Management Support

On many occasions, you need access to the broker/owner. Having a mentor is great, but if the mentor is not the broker/owner, you also need access to the broker or another decision-maker in the brokerage. You need to identify who they will be and see if they have enough time available to help you.

If a broker/owner also works on their own deals, they may be too busy to help you, so there should be someone else in a decision-making capacity that has the time to help you.

One person in a management capacity is usually not able to effectively oversee more than 40-50 agents, so if you are joining a brokerage with hundreds of agents, make sure there is a team of decision-makers available to help those agents so that you can get timely responses.

Administrative Support

Many agents are attracted to offices that provide support with paperwork. There is someone that can load the property on the MLS for you, someone to write your offers and handle your escrows. Sounds great, but this is not the way to learn the business. To know the business, you need to understand and experience each step of the process, and the process is a bit different each time you go through it. Therefore, you should do it all yourself (with your mentor's help) for the first few times. At that stage, one of two things will happen. You might realize that you want to keep doing it now that you know how to do it, or you might want to pass it on to someone else.

A brokerage may provide you an in-house person to handle your paperwork (and there is usually a cost to that, such as a specific fee or a lower split for you), or you can find endless independent transaction coordinators yourself to work with.

Brokerage Focus Area(s)

Many brokerages focus strictly on residential real estate. Some brokerages focus strictly on commercial real estate. Others handle both residential and commercial transactions.

Some residential brokerages further specialize in one or more of these areas:

- Working with seniors
- Working with investors
- Working with first time home buyers
- Working with condo owners
- Residential Leasing
- Vacation homes
- Luxury Sales
- Luxury Leasing
- Bank owned properties (REO)
- Probate properties

Commercial brokerages focus on sales, leasing, property management, or a combination of. They may further focus on one or more of the following types of commercial real estate:

- Multi-family (5+ units)
- Retail
- Industrial
- Office
- Land
- Shopping centers
- Hospitality
- Flex
- Healthcare
- Sports and entertainment
- Student housing

- Specialty (other)

Some brokerages will let you work in multiple specialization areas. Other brokerages have strict guidelines on what the office handles.

Leads and Referrals

For significant long term success, you eventually need to be able to generate your own leads. Until then, it can be of benefit to you if the brokerage provides you with leads once in a while.

Brokerages get inquiries to their website, and people call in on specific properties for sale without a particular agent in mind.

Find out who gets those leads and how it is decided. Some brokerages send them to experienced agents that are known to close deals. Other brokerages send them to the new agents to help them get started on their careers.

Learn the potential cost of leads provided by the brokerage, and remember, there is usually no free lunch.

Internet Presence

Most people use the internet and will check you and your brokerage out online. Your broker's website should be professional and up to date.

The brokerage website should be promoting the brand, the brokerage, and its agents.

Culture

At the end of the day, unless you partner with any other agents in the office and share commission, they are your competition, and you should carefully evaluate and triple-check their advice before you take it.

Are you looking for a boutique brokerage with an intimate, family-like brokerage culture? Or do you prefer a national or regional franchise brokerage where you will likely need to be on guard? Are you looking for get-togethers and brokerage caravans on open house day?

Remember, other agents, are, for the most part, your competition. Are you looking to socialize with your competition? Will they teach you what you need to know or direct you into paths on which you will spin your wheels and burn your tires?

If you love your independence and do not like corporate culture, an independent brokerage may be the way to go. The main advantage of joining a franchise is name recognition, but then the market is saturated with these names.

No matter what culture you choose, you need to enjoy being in it, which will motivate you to continue on the path.

Brokerage Size

There are advantages and disadvantages to joining large or small brokerages.

Advantages of Large Brokerages:

- You might like the energy of a large office.
- Training classes for agents may be offered.
- Brand name recognition.

Disadvantages of Large Brokerages:

- Plenty of motivational meetings that waste time and provide little benefit otherwise.
- Rigid procedures may not work for you.
- Leads coming to the brokerage likely will go to those agents that are closer to the broker.
- Not likely to accommodate new ideas.
- Their strategy is to bring in as many agents as possible and see who sticks within their environment, not to accommodate and ensure each agent's success.

Advantages of Small Brokerages:

- The cohesiveness of a smaller office environment.
- One on one mentoring and coaching for agents.
- Local brand name recognition.
- It is in their interest to make sure whoever they bring on is successful, as they do not have the time or resources to bring in masses of new agents.
- You will be working directly with the broker or a person assigned by them.
- Fewer leads will come to the brokerage, but you will have a better shot at those leads when they come in because fewer agents are around.
- Much more flexibility to discuss and implement creative ideas to grow your own business within the brokerage.

Disadvantages of Small Brokerages:

- Likely no classroom-type training
- Lack of name recognition of a big brand.

Facilities

Clients do not go into offices much if at all, these days. They expect you to come to them, meet them at properties, and for the most part, communicate with them electronically.

If you insist on joining a brokerage with an office, consider the following:

- The look of the office
- Reasonable workspace size for you
- Use of computer and copier
- After-hours access to the office
- Parking availability and cost

Location

In the world of Zoom, many would say there is no longer a need to go to the office. The time to drive, the cost of gas, wear and tear of the car, parking cost, and dry cleaning is unnecessary.

Meetings can be more effective via zoom, transaction management software allows you to eliminate the need for paperwork, mail can be sent to your home, and networking with other agents can be done via zoom. So why have an office? How often will you go there? For what reasons?

Chapter 12 – Marketing Yourself, Your Brand and Your Services

Chapter Overview

Chapter 12 explains why and how to define a unique selling proposition and a target market to focus on.

It then looks at the agent's digital footprint. It proceeds to discuss capitalizing on an agent's existing network and, much more critical, for long-term success to expand that network and capitalize on an ever-expanding network.

The chapter concludes by discussing various marketing channels utilized by agents to convey their unique selling proposition to their target market.

Chapter Outline

Your Unique Selling Proposition

Your Target Market Segment

Your Digital Footprint

Your Existing Network

Marketing to Your Existing Network

Referrals from Your Existing Network

Expanding your Network

Marketing to your Expanding Network

Marketing Channels

About Marketing Yourself, Your Brand, and Your Services

Most people that start a real estate sales career fail within one to two years. It takes time to create success in real estate. Some get lucky and close a deal within the first few months, but for many others, it may take 1-2 years or more to start generating income consistently and longer in commercial real estate.

What distinguishes many of those that do succeed from the majority that does not is their ability to stay focused and not give up. It also helps to have some money saved and/or a part or even full-time job. You will need money to live and money to invest in your business.

Investing money in your business can be in the form of joining a local board of realtors and the local multiple listing service. You should also be able to invest some money in marketing yourself, your brand, and your services.

To market yourself, you need to define what you specialize in, to clearly define your unique selling point (USP), and your target market segment.

This chapter provides a brief overview to give you a flavor of what much of your career will be about: marketing yourself, your brand, and your services. It is not the goal of this chapter to provide an in-depth, comprehensive treatment of this topic. Many books have been written on real estate marketing.

Your Unique Selling Proposition

You need to identify what makes your business unique, given so much competition all around, to target your sales efforts successfully.

For example, you can specialize in:

- Helping international buyers purchase investment properties
- Selling commercial off-market deals
- Leasing office space or any other type of property
- Helping first-time buyers
- Helping with down payment assistance programs
- Helping seniors transition to senior living
- Helping empty nesters scale down to smaller homes
- The sale of foreclosed properties (REOs)
- Short sales
- Probate sales

Your Target Market Segment

It is not practical for most new agents to effectively target a large part of the market. It is best to focus on a few thousand people in a more narrow market segment.

A few examples:

- Condo owners in a specific part of town
- Land owners in a particular area of the county

- Seniors in a specific area
- Financial Institutions that operate in your area
- Certain types of professionals (accountants, attorneys, medical doctors, etc.)
- High net worth individuals
- First time home buyers
- Owners of multiple single-family homes
- Owners of a specific type of commercial real estate in select zip codes

Your Digital Footprint

People search for you before they meet you and after they meet you. Search yourself online and see what they will see.

What should they find about you:

- Your website
- You on your broker's website
- Your LinkedIn profile
- Your other social media profiles
- Photos of you
- Videos of you
- Articles you wrote
- Articles written about you

Website

Your website should be focused on conveying your USP to your target audience.

Your website would include:

- Information about you
- Information about your services
- Your videos
- Articles you wrote or that were written about you
- Your or your broker's listings
- MLS search for all listings in the market
- News
- Contact us page

Videos

People love watching videos! You should focus on creating the following types of videos:

- Showcasing your real estate listings (or those of your broker)
- Discussing who you are and your services
- Discussing various real estate topics

- Discussing social topics you care about
- Interviewing other processionals related to your business
- Showcasing streets, neighborhoods, and businesses
- Showcasing community events

If you are short on funds, you can shoot videos yourself, have a family member or friend shoot them, or find a college student specializing in a related field to help you and gain experience in the process.

Once you create each video, upload it to YouTube, insert the YouTube link into your website, as well as on social media.

Your Existing Network

It takes time to develop relations before you can convert them to sales. An excellent place to start for many agents is their existing personal and/or professional networks. It can include the following categories of people you already know:

- Family contacts
- Friends
- Neighbors
- K-12 Classmates
- College/University contacts
- Colleagues from previous places of work
- Contacts from the places of worship you attend/attended
- Contacts from social/sports clubs you attend/attended
- Facebook and other social media friends (that are not in any of the above categories)

Marketing to Your Existing Network

Let everyone in your existing network know that you became a real estate agent and that you are happy to help them. Ask them if you can help them at this time. If they do not require your services now, ask when you should check in with them again about this.

Referrals from Your Existing Network

At a certain stage, you should ask every person you know for a referral to other people that may need your services, or that could help you grow your business.

Expanding your Network

Some new agents start their careers with a fantastic existing network and do not have a great urgency to add to this network. For most agents, however, this is not the case. Most agents are not able to significantly capitalize on their existing network. They need to expand it to the target market segment(s) they decided to pursue (as discussed earlier in this chapter).

Marketing is key to your success as a real estate agent, and marketing never ends. Think of major brands in any industry. They continuously market their products and services. You will need to do the same.

Marketing to your Expanding Network

You will need to work on defining and implementing your custom marketing campaign. It will be based on your USP and directed to your target market segment(s).

You will need to select various marketing channels, define specific campaigns for each channel, measure each campaign's effectiveness, and then adjust your future campaigns based on lessons learned.

A good broker should help you with your marketing strategy to get you going.

Marketing Channels

There are traditional marketing channels as well as online marketing channels you can select from. Experimentation will show you which works best for you.

Traditional marketing channels include:

- Advertising in paper publications
- Writing articles for paper publications
- Joining organizations, attending meetings, events
- Bench advertising
- Mailing flyers to peoples' homes
- Calling people, keeping in mind the National Do Not Call Registry

Online marketing channels include:

- Mass email
- Mass text
- Mass voice mails
- LinkedIn and other social media – to connect, communicate and post messages
- Blogging

Ultimately you must speak with people on the phone, zoom with them, and of course, meet with them to convert them to sellers and/or buyers and grow your pipeline of business.

Part Four – Additional Real Estate Careers

Part four provides a more in-depth look at additional career opportunities in and related to the real estate industry. Chapter 13 looks at real estate finance. Chapter 14 looks at property management. Chapter 15 looks at real estate auctions. Chapter 16 looks at 1031 exchanges. Chapter 17 looks at residential leasing. Chapter 18 looks at commercial leasing. Finally, Chapter 19 looks at investing in real estate.

Chapter 13 – Real Estate Finance

Chapter Overview

Chapter 13 looks at what loan officers and mortgage brokers do. It starts by providing a look at the key characteristics of loans. It then proceeds to discuss the four elements of getting a loan.

The chapter then details the financing process and concludes with a discussion of financing options.

By the end of this chapter, you should have an understanding of basic real estate finance and can decide if this is something you want to pursue as a career.

Chapter Outline

Characteristics of Loans

The Four Elements to Getting a Loan

The Financing Process

Financing Options

About Real Estate Finance

Loan officers and mortgage brokers help borrowers with the finance or refinance of their real estate assets. This chapter looks at the basic characteristics of loans, what it takes to get a loan, the financing process, and different types of financing. This will give you an idea if a real estate finance career path is or is not for you.

Loan officers, as well as mortgage brokers, are referred to as lenders in this chapter.

Characteristics of Loans

Interest Rate

Different loans have different interest rates. Generally, the longer the term, the higher the interest rate.

Amortization

Fully amortized loans – Borrower pays principal and interest each month, and by the end of the term, the loan is fully paid off.

Partially amortized loans – Borrower pays principal and interest each month. The amount paid does not result in the loan being fully paid off at the end of the term. There is a final payment to pay the difference called "balloon payment".

Interest Only Loans – Borrower pays interest only for the duration or portion of the loan duration. There is a balloon payment at the end of the term.

Repayment Period

Most often, loans are for 30-year terms. However, there are also loans for 15 and 20-year terms available to borrowers. The longer the term, if all other characteristics are the same, then the smaller are the monthly payments.

Loan to Value (LTV)

Loan to Value (LTV) is a ratio of the loan amount vs. the property's purchase price. For example, an LTV of 90% means that on a $1,000,000 purchase, the buyer pays $100,000 from their funds, and the lender finances the rest ($900,000).

The lower the LTV, the less risky the loan is for lenders. Different loan programs have different maximum LTV requirements.

Mortgage Insurance

Lenders typically require mortgage insurance for loans with higher LTV value and/or borrowers with lower credit scores.

Secondary Financing
> Loan to pay part of the down payment for the first loan and/or the closing costs.

Fixed vs. Adjustable-Rate Loans
> The interest rate remains the same for fixed-rate loans. For Adjustable-Rate Loans (ARM), the lender can adjust the interest rate, depending on a specific index.

The Four Elements to Getting a Loan
> The four elements lenders take into consideration when approving a loan are (see Figure 35):

- Credit (including liabilities and credit history)
- Income
- Assets
- Property to be Acquired

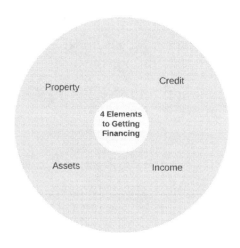

Figure 35 - Four Elements to Getting Financing

The Financing Process
> The financing process consists of possible pre-qualification, pre-approval, conditional commitment, locking the rate and terms, and finally financing the property. The process is outlined in Figure 36.

Figure 36 - The Financing Process

Each step in the process is further discussed below.

Pre-Qualification

A buyer approaches a lender to get general information about the loan process and qualification guidelines. This step requires the buyer to verbally provide financial attributes to the lender to determine which loan program is the best fit for a hypothetical purchase price. The potential loan amount and monthly payments are discussed for the buyer to self-determine affordability and sufficient funds with no application or verification completed.

The "pre-qualification" is often used interchangeably with the "pre-approval," so it is highly recommended to get clarification when discussing this with real estate professionals or buyers.

Pre-Approval

This step is more common, making the pre-qualification process obsolete. This process requires the buyer(s) to complete a loan application (usually online or by phone) and authorize the lender to order a credit report to review outstanding liabilities and payment history. The lender then reviews the financial attributes, clarifies employment history and source of down payment and closing costs in the application to ensure accuracy, and then generates an automated disposition in minutes by sending encrypted financial data electronically to Desktop Underwriter or a similar automated underwriting system to approve or decline the application. This process allows the lender to provide the buyer with a pre-approval letter or advance the application to an underwriter for confirmation if the automated system recommends a decline decision.

Conditional Commitment Letter

This is the highest and best step to take, where the lender can provide the buyer with a conditional commitment letter. This is an upgrade to the pre-approval letter. This process requires the borrower to provide the lender with documentation to validate the pre-approval application's financial attributes. This consists of providing the lender the check stubs, W2s, tax returns, and bank, retirement, and investment account statements as needed to comply with loan program guidelines. The lender's underwriter then reviews this documentation to upgrade pre-approval to full approval subject to purchase contract and third-party documentation from vendors providing title and escrow services.

Formal Loan Approval

By the time buyer successfully negotiates the purchase contract, the Conditional Commitment Letter can transition to Loan Approval Letter after escrow and title documentation is reviewed by the underwriter, provided the credit report and income/asset documentation haven't expired. Should any document be about to expire during the escrow period, the buyer should provide the lender with updated documentation making it critical not to get into additional debt and not lose work or get paid less after the loan application is pre-approved. Usually, the loan rate and terms can be locked at this time to ensure the loan approval is stable throughout the escrow period; the Loan Estimate that details the potential closing costs is issued, and the appraisal report is ordered.

Final Loan Approval

Final loan approval occurs after the underwriter reviews the complete file consisting of the fully executed purchase contract package, escrow instructions, preliminary title report, appraisal report, verbal verification of continued employment by a third-party vendor, and updated customer documentation (if necessary) to ensure data is current and in compliance with loan program guidelines. The file is now considered "cleared to close", with the underwriter no longer involved in the closing process.

Funding the Property

The last step in the financing process is getting the loan funded after the file is "cleared to close". However, before the buyer can sign loan documents, the buyer must acknowledge the Closing Disclosure (CD) to confirm the final accounting of closing costs is acceptable. The CD prepared by the lender summarizes the final accounting for all non-recurring and recurring closing costs associated with the home's purchase. The accounting is a collaboration between the lender and escrow, providing detail on the actual costs to close. Federal laws require the CD to be acknowledged by the buyer at least three days before signing loan documents, so this step is crucial for closing on time.

If the accounting is in error for any reason, releasing a new CD can delay closing until the new three-day time period has passed. Assuming the final accounting is within legal parameters from what was on the Loan Estimate when the purchase contract was provided, the buyer signs the loan documents after three days pass. Then later, the same day or next, the escrow company faxes/emails copy of signed loan documents to the lender with the proof they received the balance of funds needed to close the transaction from the buyer, and the lender funds the loan the same day.

Financing Options

A variety of financing options are available for a buyer interested in submitting an offer for a property. The following sections describe these types of financing, as well as others that are available for buyers (see Figure 37).

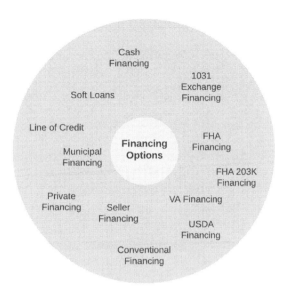

Figure 37 - Types of Real Estate Financing

Conventional Financing

Conventional loans are perhaps the most common type of financing used by buyers. Conventional loans usually require 20% down, an appraisal substantiating the loan to value ratio, and specific habitability requirements related to the property's condition. Still, relative to an FHA loan, these conditions are usually few and liberal.

If the down payment is (typically) less than 20%, mortgage insurance may be required and could increase the monthly payment.

Individual lenders may have additional property requirements that other lenders may not have. For example, some lenders may require Section 1 Termite clearance while others do not. Conventional loans typically take up to 30 days to fund.

Cash, Hard Money, and Line of Credit Financing

When a buyer specifies that they are offering "Cash", the listing agent must review the buyer's proof of funds to ensure that funds are sufficient, liquid, and dated within the past 30 days. Cash offers are usually the most appealing to sellers because funds are immediately available, and the offer does not carry a loan contingency. For cash offers, liquid funds can be transferred to the closing company within a day if desired.

Examples of liquid funds include funds held in a bank and investments like stocks and Certificate of Deposits (CDs). For investments, you must consider potential penalties and value losses if the buyer withdraws funds. If a fee is assessed for withdrawing funds, you must ensure that funds are still sufficient for purchase.

If a buyer is obtaining a "Hard Money Loan" or a "Line of Credit" aka "HELOC," and their offer is one of the strongest, you should contact the lender and buyer. Identify the type of documentation that has been reviewed by the lender, what the loan is contingent upon, is the line of credit based on home equity that the lender may withdraw, etc.?

Although buyers' agents designate them as "cash", these offers are not cash. Listing agents should also inquire how much of a down payment the buyer is offering and request proof of funds for that down payment.

FHA Financing

FHA loans are mortgages insured and backed by the Federal Housing Administration (FHA) and are issued by FHA approved lenders. These loans require a lower down payment and lower credit scores than conventional loans. Their qualifying guidelines are designed to accommodate low and moderate-income borrowers. They usually require as little as 3.5% down. This type of loan is prevalent among first-time homebuyers and typically takes 45 days to fund. These loans typically require paying for mortgage insurance as well as part of the loan.

FHA loans require that an appraiser inspect the property to appraise it and identify any health and safety issues.

FHA buyer qualifications change from time to time, as governments may wish to make homes more or less accessible to buyers at different times. For example, in the past, FHA loans required Section 1 Termite Repairs to be completed and an operable stove to be installed before the close of escrow.

Note: FHA offers on properties with an HOA (Homeowners Association) cannot be considered unless the HOA is FHA approved. It is imperative to determine if an HOA is FHA approved as early as possible in the process. Sometimes the HOA's records may be outdated and will not indicate FHA approval.

If an HOA does not indicate FHA approval, check the US Department of Housing and Urban Development (HUD) website to see if the complex is FHA approved. It is the absolute authority on this matter. Housing and Urban Development (HUD) website: https://entp.hud.gov/idapp/html/condlook.cfm

FHA 203K Financing

An FHA 203K loan is a renovation mortgage sponsored by the Federal Housing Administration (FHA).

An FHA 203K loan enables buyers to finance a home's purchase and the cost to rehabilitate it. A portion of the loan is used to pay the seller for the purchase, and the remaining funds are placed in an escrow account and released to the vendor(s) as renovations/repairs are completed.

The appraisal process for an FHA 203K loan is relatively long as all repairs must first be assessed. Costs for each repair or renovation must be estimated, and then buyer must qualify for the mortgage to cover these costs. The buyer selects a 203(k) consultant and a general contractor to work with and submits documentation listing repairs to be made, which is provided to the appraiser to provide an "as-repaired appraisal", which is an estimate of the fair market value after the property has been repaired.

There is no need to wait for the repairs to be completed before the lender will fund the transaction. The lengthy appraisal process means these loans typically take 45-60 days to close.

VA Financing

This type of financing is guaranteed by the United States Department of Veterans Affairs (VA) for qualified veterans of military service. VA loans typically require no down payment (0% down) and include lender terms and conditions comparable to an FHA loan. VA loans usually take 30-60 days to fund.

USDA Financing

This type of financing is guaranteed by the United States Department of Agriculture (USDA) for individuals purchasing homes in rural and certain pockets of suburban areas. The USDA guarantees mortgages issued by participating lenders. The USDA also issues loans directly to low and very-low-income applicants. They are low-interest mortgages with zero down payment.

The purpose of these loans is to promote ownership in defined rural areas of the country to drive community development in agricultural areas. Income qualification for this type of loan is capped at 150% of the median income for that area.

Many lenders are reluctant to offer loans for these markets because they present a high-risk to the lender. Properties in these markets may quickly lose significant value due to severe weather, unstable dependence on local companies, and other events that can devastate local economies.

The USDA's home financing program is designed to compensate for this market gap/risk aversion. These loans include lender terms and conditions comparable to an FHA loan. USDA loans usually take 30-60 days to fund.

1031 Exchange Financing

The buyer obtains funding for this type of financing by selling a property that they previously owned. Funds from the sale are usually held by a qualified intermediary and can be used to purchase a different property.

1031 exchange is defined under section 1031 of the IRS Code. A 1031 exchange allows an investor to defer paying capital gains taxes on an investment property when it is sold, as long as another like-kind property is purchased with the funds from the first property's sale.

1031 exchange is discussed in more detail later in Chapter 16.

Seller Financing

In seller financing, the seller assumes the role of a lender. The seller extends credit to the buyer for the purchase, less the down payment. Buyer and seller sign a promissory note. They record a mortgage or deed of trust with the public recorder's office. The majority of these loans are short-term, with a balloon payment due in, say, five years.

The idea is that within a few years, the home will have gained enough in value, or the buyers' financial situation would have improved so that the buyer can refinance with a traditional lender.

Private Financing

Private lenders are not affiliated with a bank or other financial institution. Private lenders use their capital to finance real estate purchases and work directly with the borrower. Investors or banks or both generally fund them. They provide short-term loans to investors for the purchase or renovation of investment properties.

Private loans are usually processed much faster than other types of loans and have more lenient buyer qualification criteria, may not have appraisal contingencies, and are generally only offered to well-established investor buyers.

Many buyer's agents refer to these loans as cash on their offers, but they are not cash. This type of financing still has qualifying criteria, and most of the time, requires a down payment from the buyer.

Private lenders are still subject to state and federal law but are significantly less regulated and can be more flexible in the types of loans they can make and who they choose to lend to.

Line of Credit

Buyers may wish to finance their offer with a line of credit. The most common line of credit is the Home Equity Line of Credit (HELOC). HELOC loans are based on the difference between your current home's value and your current mortgage balance.

Buyers' agents often present lines of credit as cash, but they are not cash. The possibility that a line of credit may be revoked due to depreciating property values or other reasons also means that a line of credit is not a dependable source of funds.

Other lines of credit include lines extended to investors by capital groups. While these capital groups do have the cash to pay, and the line of credit is more or less assured, these financing types often carry "subject to appraisal" or "back-end buyer needed" conditions.

Still, most lines of credit rank higher than conventional or FHA loans in sellers' eyes because a line of credit funds faster and carries fewer conditions than a conventional or FHA loan.

Soft Loans

Soft loans are usually provided by government entities or nonprofit organizations and often do not require the buyer to repay the loan until the buyer resells the property. Some entities require that low levels of interest accrue over this period (usually, these rates are comparable with inflation figures), while others charge no interest at all.

Municipal Financing

Typically, municipal loans are designated for Neighborhood Stabilization Programs (NSP). These are designed to draw homeowners into areas with a high volume of rented properties and communities municipal governments would like to see improved. It is assumed that homeowners will have a greater vested interest in improving these communities than the tenants of rented properties.

There are usually caps on municipal loans, required concessions, and limitations on which properties can qualify. For example, some municipal loans may only be offered on foreclosed homes.

Municipal loans for Neighborhood Stabilization (NSP) programs are usually a type of soft loan that gives homeowners an incentive to choose a property in less desirable neighborhoods. The caps on these loans typically mean they are used more like a second loan in addition to a buyer's first loan.

Other municipal loans are city or county backed loans. These loans are usually designated only for specific properties, specific blocks, or particular buildings that the city or county wishes to develop or restore.

Chapter 14 - Property Management

Chapter Overview

Chapter 14 provides a look at what property managers do. It starts by signing a management contract and then defining and deploying takeover procedures.

It looks at the ongoing reporting relationship with the owners, establishing rents, marketing properties for lease, screening tenants, negotiating leases, helping tenants move in, collecting rents, renewing leases, handling tenant issues as they arise, and assisting tenants with moveouts.

The chapter concludes with a discussion about handling legal matters, performing regular inspections, handling maintenance, repairs, and remodeling, and of course, handling financial matters and reporting those to the owners.

By the end of this chapter, you should have a basic understanding of property management and can decide if this is something you want to pursue as a career.

Chapter Outline

- Define and Sign a Management Contract
- Define and Deploy Takeover Procedures
- Ongoing Relationship with Owner/Representative
- Evaluate the Property to Establish Rents
- Market the Property for Lease
- Tenant Screening, Selection, and Lease Negotiations
- Tenant Move-In
- Rent Collection
- Lease Renewals
- Tenant Relations
- Tenant Move Out
- Tenancy Termination
- Legal
- Inspections
- Financial Reporting
- Maintenance, Repair, Remodeling

About Property Management

Many owners of commercial assets choose to hire professional property managers or management companies to manage their real estate assets. Consider property management as a system that involves many components that work together to achieve a common goal. It takes a detail-oriented person to see and be able to oversee the big picture.

Knowing property management can help you manage your properties as well one day.

This chapter provides an overview of the various activities property managers handle (See Figure 38 below).

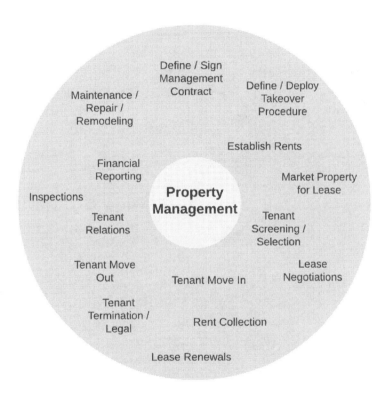

Figure 38 - Key Property Management Activities

Key property management activities are discussed in the following sections.

Define and Sign a Management Contract

You should work with your client to define and sign an agreement to manage and lease real estate. A real estate management contract typically includes:

- The parties to the contract
- The duration of the contract

- Authority and responsibilities of the management company (you)
- Responsibilities of the owner
- Exclusions
- Termination
- Fees
- Signatures

Define and Deploy Takeover Procedures

Once the management contract is signed, it is time to transfer responsibilities. You should request all data necessary for the efficient operation of the property.

Ongoing Relationship with Owner/Representative

You should provide your client with monthly reports, including financial reports. You should keep an open communication channel with them, informing them of any issues that require their attention as they arise.

Evaluate the Property to Establish Rents

You should conduct a property and market analysis, provide you with lease values of comparable properties in the vicinity of the subject property and make a recommendation of likely lease price(s).

Market the Property for Lease

You should prepare the property for lease, which may include cleanup and/or remodeling. The next steps include marketing the property using traditional and online marketing strategies, handling showings to prospective tenants, and providing and collecting applications.

Tenant Screening, Selection, and Lease Negotiations

You should provide each prospective tenant with a lease application and run credit and background checks if they consent to it. There are several excellent online applications on the market that can help you with tenant screening. The prospective tenant typically pays for the service. Chapter 17 provides additional details on tenant screening and lease negotiations.

Tenant Move-In

Once you have identified a qualified tenant, you should complete a leasing agreement, confirm the move-in date with the tenant, review lease guidelines with the tenant, and ensure all agreements have been properly executed.

You should use the C.A.R Residential Lease/Month-to-Month Rental Agreement (LR) form for residential leases. For commercial leases, you should use the C.A.R. Commercial Lease Agreement (CL) or the AIR CRE Contracts, based on the property type.

Once there is a fully executed lease, you should collect the first month's rent and the security deposit and conduct a walkthrough of the property with the tenant(s). You should use the C.A.R. MIMO form to document the move-in condition of each item listed on the form, either as new, satisfactory/clean, or other, and comments should be noted to explain the condition. Photos should be taken as well during the move-in walkthrough to document the condition of the property. The tenant(s) should review, initial, and sign the form, and you should provide it to the owner for review, initials, and signature as well.

Rent Collection

You or the owner will be collecting rents, pursuing late payments, issuing notices to pay rent or quit, and enforcing late fees.

Typically you or the owner should maintain three trust accounts (for properties with a large number of tenants):

- Operating account
- Reserve fund account
- Security deposit account

Lease Renewals

Steady tenants with a good payment history are assets. The quality of your tenants and existing market conditions will dictate the parameters of a lease extension. To extend the term of an existing lease, you can use the C.A.R. Extension of Lease (EL) form. Any new or modified terms can be specified on this form.

Tenant Relations

You should maintain a good relationship with the tenant(s). You might check in with them periodically to see how things are going. You should be responsive within reason to their requests.

Tenant Move Out

Once the tenant(s) are ready to move out, you should conduct a move out walkthrough with the tenant(s) and use and document findings in the C.A.R. MIMO form. Look for changes in property condition at move-in, and take photos to document each change. The "move out" column should be completed, specifying the condition of each item listed as either satisfactory or requiring a deposit deduction, and comments should be noted. The tenant will review, initial, and sign the "Move Out" section of the form, and it should be provided to the owner for initial and signature as well. Provide the tenant with a copy of the fully executed MIMO form and calculate any withholdings. Before returning the security deposit, subtract the cost of repairs and explain to the tenant(s) what will be withheld from their deposit and why. The unit should have sales cleaning performed, and any necessary repairs made, and the property should be rekeyed. You should market the property to identify the next qualified tenant.

Tenancy Termination

A lease may expire, and the tenant may not wish to extend the lease. In the event a quality tenant wishes to leave the property, you should try to understand why this is happening and see if they can reverse the decision by asking what the reason is for termination.

If the tenant insists on moving on, the security deposit should be returned, less the portion kept for damages.

A tenant may abandon the property, a tenant may surrender the property by mutual agreement, or the tenant may be evicted (as discussed in Chapter 5).

Legal

You should understand and abide by the latest local, state, and federal laws that apply to leasing and maintaining rental properties. You should consult with a qualified attorney if and when necessary.

Inspections

You should perform periodic inspections looking for health and safety hazards, code violations, lease violations, and other things that may require repairs. You should send the owner periodic reports on the condition of the property.

Financial Reporting

You (if applicable) should provide accounting property management services and make payments on the owner's behalf. Ongoing monthly, quarterly, and annual reporting should be provided.

Maintenance, Repair, Remodeling

You should have a network of licensed, bonded, and fully insured vendors who have been vetted for good quality work and reasonable pricing. You should assign jobs to different parties based on who will do the best job for the best price. You should maintain and monitor a 24-hour emergency repair hotline. You could also oversee more extensive renovation or rehab projects.

Specialized property management companies tend to create plans that include:

- Ongoing maintenance
- Preventative maintenance
- Handling maintenance requests
- Routine inspections

Chapter 15 - Real Estate Auction

Chapter Overview

Chapter 15 presents the benefits of auction and the differences between auction sales and standard real estate sales. The chapter then proceeds to look at different types of auctions. Next, the chapter details the various steps of the auction process.

The chapter concludes with a look at some specific scenarios common to auctions of real estate assets.

By the end of this chapter, you should have a basic understanding of real estate auctions and can decide if this is something you want to pursue as a career.

Chapter Outline

Benefits of Real Estate Auction

Differences Between Ordinary Sales and Auction Sales

Auctions with Reserve

Auctions Subject to Seller Confirmation

Absolute Auction / Auction without Reserve

Important Terms of the Auction Contract

Bidder Registration

Terms Included in Auction Advertising

Due Diligence Prior to Auction

Switch to Auction if Can Not Sell via Ordinary Sale?

Auction Sale for Occupied Property with No Interior Access?

About Real Estate Auctions

Auctioning real estate properties is not something most agents handle, but depending on your personality and communication skills may be of interest. Auctions are very popular in some parts of the US and relatively rare in others.

Going once, going twice.... Sold! These statements are what make auctions fun and exciting. An auction is generally a public sale of property to the highest bidder conducted by an auctioneer. The auctioneer's goal is to obtain the best financial return for the seller by free and fair competition among bidders.

Some define real estate auction as the public sale of real estate, in which the sale price offered is increased by competitive bids until the highest accepted bidder becomes the purchaser. Competitive bidding is a fundamental part of real estate auctions. It's the competition that pushes the price up, higher and higher.

Benefits of Real Estate Auction

There are multiple important benefits to conducting a real estate auction (see Figure 39). These include:

- The seller knows when the property will sell
- The seller sets a reserve price and does not need to be involved in the negotiations process
- Buyers arrive ready to purchase the property
- Includes a comprehensive marketing program that maximizes interest and visibility
- Exposes the property to a large number of pre-approved prospective buyers
- Requires potential buyers to pre-qualify for financing
- Accelerates the sale
- Reduces ongoing carrying costs, including taxes and maintenance, due to quick disposal
- Creates excitement leading to increased competition among buyers, which can result in auction price exceeding the price of a negotiated sale
- Ensures that property will be sold at true market value

Figure 39 - Benefits of Real Estate Auction

Differences Between Ordinary Sales and Auction Sales

In an Ordinary Sale:

- The seller does not know exactly when the property will sell.
- The seller can set a reserve price in their mind but needs to be involved in the negotiation process.
- The sale can include a comprehensive marketing program that maximizes interest and visibility
    - However, most agents simply place the property on the MLS, and from there, it automatically propagates to other websites such as Zillow.
- Present the property to a large number of prospective buyers, which may or may not be qualified.
- It can require potential buyers to be vetted, providing financing pre-approval and proof of funds; however, many agents do not do that.
- Some buyers that submit offers are ready to purchase, while others are not.
- The sale can be accelerated if the property is listed at the bottom of the comps or below the comps.
- Quick disposal is possible if the property is priced at the bottom or below the comps, thus reducing long term carrying costs.
    - However, most agents do not list at the bottom or below the comps.
- Some buzz and excitement leading to increased competition among buyers can be created.
    - Price property very competitively.

- o Set a quick deadline to submit offers.
- o As soon as the second offer comes in, inform everyone there is a multiple offer situation.
- o As soon as the first offer above the asking price comes in, start informing everyone you have offers above ask.
- o As soon as the first cash offer comes in, start informing everyone your offers include all-cash offers.

As you can see, it is possible to simulate excitement and competition similar to that created in an auction by conducting ordinary sales using the right strategies. However, for various reasons, most agents are not able to accomplish this.

Auctions with Reserve

An "auction with reserve" is an auction where the seller establishes a reserve on a property and is subject to the seller's confirmation – sellers are not obligated to confirm a sale other than at a price that's acceptable to them. The reserve is the minimum price that a seller is willing to accept for the property to be sold at auction. In an auction with a reserve, the property offered will sell to the highest bidder only if the auctioneer accepts the highest bid and declares the property sold.

The auctioneer is not required to disclose the reserve price at the auction and generally doesn't do so. The seller reserves the right to accept or reject the highest bid within a specified time. Once a bid is submitted that exceeds the reserve price, the property can be sold to the highest bidder. The auctioneer can announce that the reserve has been met, and the property will sell today in an effort to generate more bids. This type of auction reduces the seller's risk since the sales price must be above a minimum acceptable level.

Potential buyers may not invest the time and money in due diligence in reserve auctions since there is no certainty they will be able to buy the property even if they are the highest bidder. This type of auction limits interest to those buyers willing to pay the minimum bid price, and so has to be low enough to attract bidders.

For example, your seller wants to sell real property and believes its value is $1,000,000. If they do not want to risk selling the property for less than it is worth, you can place a reserve on it. The auctioneer should assist the seller in establishing the reserve. In this instance, the auctioneer may establish a reserve price of $950,000. The reserve will prevent that property from being sold for an amount less than $950,000. You can reject the bids or withdraw the property if bids come in lower than $950,000.

Auctions Subject to Seller Confirmation

At an auction that is subject to the seller's confirmation, the seller does not establish a minimum bid or reserve. Instead, they simply reserve the right to reject any and all bids regardless of price or justification. The auctioneer will present them with the highest bid made for the property after the bidding. They will then decide whether to accept the bid and sell the property or not.

There is no certainty as to the selling price. The seller can accept the highest bid or reject it. Until the highest bid is received, the seller does not need to make any specific determination. This type of sale can be used for any kind of property but may be particularly helpful when it is difficult to determine the property's value. This would reduce the risk of setting the reserve either too high or too low.

Absolute Auction / Auction without Reserve

In an absolute auction or an auction held without reserve, the property is sold to the highest bidder, regardless of the price. This type of sale generates the maximum response from the market, and buyer excitement and participation are heightened.

Mutual contingent assent is achieved when an offer is made. Each bid made is a mutual assent between the seller and the respective bidder, contingent only on no higher bid being received. As each high bid is made, the previous contract is extinguished, and a new contract based on mutual contingent assent comes into being. When no further bids are made, the last bid's contingency is extinguished, and a final contract in the series of contingent contracts is established.

Therefore, absolute auctions are not marketed as subject to seller confirmation, lender approval, financing, minimum bid, or anything else. An absolute auction is a sale to the highest bidder with no limiting conditions.

This has its risks. Some believe real property should be sold subject to any liens at a reserve auction. The owner and the auctioneer should discuss setting the reserve price at an amount that will allow the owner to pay the balance owed for any lien and/or mortgage. An auction with a reserve will assure the owner that they will not be responsible for paying the difference between the selling price and the amount owed on the mortgage or lien. It is discouraged to approve the sale of property with a mortgage, or any type of lien on it, at an auction without reserve.

Important Terms of the Auction Contract

The key terms of an auction contract include:

- Exclusive right to sell the property
- Address of the property to be sold
- Term/duration of the contract
- Place, time, and date of the auction
- Auctioneer's duties and obligations
- Whether the sale is with or without reserve
- If there is a specific reserve, the reserve amount
- Authority of the auctioneer to act on behalf of the seller
- Authority of the auctioneer to charge a buyer's premium
- Acceptable methods of payment
- Seller's duties and obligations
- Liability for damage to property
- Sellers's representations and warranties (Clear title, ability, and authority to sell)

- Description of the property to be used at the auction
- Seller's acknowledgment of risk in the sales
- Liens and encumbrances
- Compensation of auctioneer (commission)
- Payment of expenses (e.g., advertisement costs)
- Arbitration clauses or alternative dispute resolution terms
- Other miscellaneous provisions

Bidder Registration

Bidders are required to register for the auction before the sale. The registration process clarifies the terms of the sale contract. When bidders register, they typically show their driver's license or another form of identity, provide contract information, and execute a document containing the sale's essential terms. By executing the registration agreement, the bidder accepts the terms and conditions of the sale and agrees to be bound by them. The terms and conditions outlined in the registration form should supplement and complement any terms announced by the auctioneer before the sale. After registering for the sale, the bidder is provided with a bid card and bid number.

Terms Included in Auction Advertising

Specific terms should be included in an auction advertisement. These items include: (1) the time, place, and date of the auction; (2) general description of the property or lots to be sold; (3) any disclaimer of warranties; (4) notice that a buyer's premium will be charged, if any, and the percentage amount; (5) any deposit requirements; and (6) in a minimum bid auction, the minimum price should be stated.

Included should be information that could help prevent a dispute. For example, an advertisement could notify the public that the seller has the right to withdraw the property from the sale or cancel the sale. This will help protect the seller and reduce the likelihood of complaints or litigation due to the withdrawal of property or the sale's cancellation.

In addition, the advertisement could give notice that the property is being sold as-is. The ad's information would help prevent others from arguing that they did not know the property was being sold without any warranties or in an "as is" condition.

Due Diligence Prior to Auction

To avoid liability, auctioneers must know what they are selling. As part of the due diligence for a real estate sale, the title search verifies that the seller owns the property and identifies any liens. The liens that may be found during a title search include, for example, mortgages, mechanic's liens, judgment liens, and tax liens. These items will usually need to be resolved before the closing.

In some instances, auctioneers ask for a property survey to provide additional clarity of what is being sold. A survey of the parcel will reveal any encroachments on the property and verify the acreage. Encroachments can include easements, disputed property lines, fence issues, and improperly installed driveways.

Switch to Auction if Can Not Sell via Ordinary Sale?

If you are unable to sell a property via ordinary sale, you could consider an auction. You can also make a massive price reduction that will, at the right price, bring lots of offers, including offers over ask if you underprice the market.

Alternatively, you can perform a series of quick smaller price reductions (weekly, for example) until offers start coming in.

If you need the money asap, preparing for and properly marketing an upcoming auction may take 30 days. Once in escrow with a cash buyer, a minimum of a couple of weeks may be requested. The same can be accomplished via an ordinary sale where the property is placed on the MLS if the list price is substantially below the market to quickly attract a large audience.

Auction Sale for Occupied Property with No Interior Access?

Before jumping to sell with no interior access, ask, why is there no interior access? You might get immediate interior access if you provide the tenant with a 24 hour Notice to Enter. Interior access for showings and inspections will provide a greater return on the sale of the property. You can also attempt to negotiate Cash for Keys with the occupant if rent is not being paid and get the property vacant.

Chapter 16 - 1031 Exchange

Chapter Overview

Chapter 16 looks at what 1031 exchange specialists do. It outlines the reasons to participate in a 1031 exchange. It then discusses what can be exchanged.

The chapter concludes with a discussion about each of the four types of exchanges and explains various 1031 exchange rules.

By the end of this chapter, you should have a basic understanding of 1031 exchanges and can decide if this is something you want to pursue as a career.

Chapter Outline

Reasons to Do a 1031 Exchange

What Can be Exchanged

Types of Real Estate Exchanges

Simultaneous 1031 Exchange

Reverse 1031 Exchange

Construction or Improvement 1031 Exchange

1031 Exchange Rules

About 1031 Exchanges

A 1031 Exchange is a powerful tax-deferment strategy used by real estate investors, which you might be able to turn into a career.

The term 1031 Exchange is defined under section 1031 of the IRS Code. This strategy allows an investor to defer paying capital gains taxes on an investment property when it is sold, as long as another like-kind property is purchased with the first property's sale proceeds.

Basic definitions:

- **Exchanger** - investor pursuing 1031 exchange strategy
- **Relinquished Property** – property sold via a 1031 exchange
- **Replacement Property** – property acquired via a 1031 exchange

Reasons to Participate in a 1031 Exchange

The following are key reasons for property owners to pursue a 1031 exchange:

- Defer payment of capital gains taxes
- Shift real estate investments from one type of real estate to another
- Diversify investment portfolios

What Can be Exchanged

1031 exchanges can be applied to different situations. Key among them are:

- Commercial real estate (office, retail, shopping centers, industrial, etc.)
- Residential units used to produce income (under very specific rules)
- Rental units that are part of primary residences
- Vacation homes (under very specific rules)

Types of Real Estate Exchanges

There are four types of 1031 Exchanges:

- Simultaneous exchange
- Delayed exchange
- Reverse exchange
- Construction exchange

A summary of each of these types of exchanges is presented next.

Simultaneous 1031 Exchange

A simultaneous exchange occurs when the replacement property and relinquished property close on the same day.

The exchange must occur simultaneously; any delay can result in the exchange's disqualification and make the seller pay the capital gains taxes on the sale.

There are three ways that a simultaneous exchange can occur:

- A swap or a two-party trade, where the parties exchange (swap) deeds with one another.
- A three-party exchange where an "accommodating party" is used to facilitate the transaction.
- Simultaneous exchange with a Qualified Intermediary (QI) who structures the exchange.

Delayed 1031 Exchange

A delayed exchange is the most common type of exchange, allowing up to a maximum of 180 days to purchase a replacement property. A qualified intermediary must be engaged to complete a delayed exchange. The three steps of a delayed 1031 exchange are detailed next (see Figure 40).

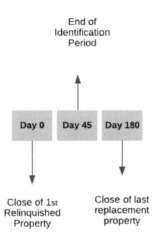

Figure 40 - Delayed Exchange Timeline

Sale of the Relinquished Property

Before closing the sale of the relinquished property, the exchanger must enter into an exchange agreement with a qualified intermediary. Based on the exchange agreement, an assignment is executed before closing, and the qualified intermediary assumes the exchanger's Purchase and Sale agreement. The QI instructs the escrow officer to deed the property from the exchanger to the buyer directly. Proceeds are transferred directly to the QI, thus protecting the exchanger from receipt of funds.

Identification of Replacement Property

The exchanger must identify potential replacement properties within 45 calendar days. The identification must be made in writing, and the property must be clearly described. The three rules of identification are:

- **Three Property Rule**: An exchanger can identify a maximum of three (3) replacement properties without regard to the properties' fair market value.
- **Two-Hundred Percent Rule**: The exchanger can identify any number of properties as long as the combined fair market value does not exceed two-hundred percent (200%) of the fair market value of the relinquished property.
- **Ninety-Five Percent Exception**: The exchanger can identify any number of properties with the combined fair market value exceeding 200%, as long as the properties acquired amount to at least ninety-five percent (95%) of the fair market value of all these identified properties.

Purchase of Replacement Property

The exchanger has 180 calendar days from the closing of the relinquished property to acquire like-kind replacement properties. Before closing on the replacement property, the exchanger assigns the Purchase and Sale Agreement to the qualified intermediary. The qualified intermediary then purchases the replacement property with the exchange funds and transfers it back to the exchanger by a direct deed from the seller.

Reverse 1031 Exchange

A reverse 1031 exchange, also known as a forward exchange, occurs when the exchanger acquires a replacement property through a QI before exchanging the property they currently own.

The exchanger has 45 days to identify what property is going to be sold as the relinquished property.

After the initial 45 days, the exchanger has 135 days to complete the sale of the identified property and complete the reverse 1031 exchange with the replacement property's purchase.

Construction or Improvement 1031 Exchange

The construction exchange allows the exchanger to make improvements on the replacement property by using the exchange equity. The exchanger can use their tax-deferred dollars to enhance the replacement property while it is in the hands of a qualified intermediary during the 180 days.

This type of exchange has three rules:

- The entire exchange equity must be spent on completed improvements and/or a down payment during the 180 days.
- The exchanger must receive "substantially the same property" that they identified by day 45.
- The replacement property must be equal or greater in value when it is deeded back to the exchanger. The improvements must be in place before the exchanger can take the title back from the QI.

1031 Exchange Rules

There are several rules to follow when exchanging properties. These rules are presented next (See Figure 41).

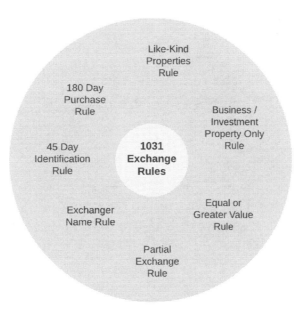

Figure 41 - 1031 Exchange Rules

Exchanging Like-Kind Properties Rule

To qualify as a 1031 exchange, the relinquished property and the replacement property must be like-kind. Like-Kind property means that both the original and replacement properties must be of "the same nature or character, even if they differ in grade or quality".

1031 Exchanges can include more than two properties. For example, the exchanger can exchange one property for multiple replacement properties or exchange multiple properties for one property.

- Any type of real property, except for a person's primary residence, can qualify for a tax-deferred exchange. However, the rules for exchanges require that the relinquished property and the replacement property are "like-kind" to one another.
- "Like-kind" does not mean that the relinquished property and the replacement property must share the same physical characteristics. For example, a shopping center does not need to be exchanged for another shopping center. It can be exchanged for an industrial warehouse, an apartment building, etc.
- "Like-kind" refers to the requirement that property be "held for investment or for productive use in a trade or business" must be exchanged for other property that is also "held for investment or for productive use in a trade or business."

Business or Investment Property Only Rule

A 1031 exchange is only applicable for business or investment property. It does not apply to personal property. Also, you can not exchange one primary residence for another.

Equal or Greater Value Rule

To defer paying 100% of the taxes for the sale of a property, the IRS requires the net market value and equity of the replacement property to be the same as or greater than the relinquished property.

Partial 1031 Exchange Rule

The exchanger can carry out a partial 1031 exchange, in which the replacement property is of lesser value, but this will not be 100% tax-free. The difference is the amount the exchanger will have to pay capital gains taxes on. This option makes sense when a seller wants to get some cash-out and is willing to pay some taxes to do so.

Exchanger Name Rule

The name appearing on the relinquished property title must be the same as the name on the tax return and the same as that of the titleholder buying the replacement property. However, a single-member LLC can sell the relinquished property, and that sole member may purchase the replacement property in their name.

45 Day Identification Window Rule

The exchanger has 45 calendar days, after closing of the relinquished property, to identify (in writing and provide documentation to the QI) one or more replacement properties, based on the three rules (3 Properties rule, 200% rule, and the 95% rule) discussed earlier in this chapter.

180 Day Purchase Window

It is necessary that the replacement property is received and the exchange completed no later than 180 days after the sale of the relinquished property or the due date of the income tax return (with extensions) for the tax year in which the relinquished property was sold, whichever is earlier.

Chapter 17 - Residential Leasing

Chapter Overview

Chapter 17 looks at some of what residential agents do. It introduces the steps involved in the residential leasing process. It looks at the possible terms of the lease and commission. It proceeds to discuss property marketing and showings.

The chapter proceeds to discuss tenant screening, the lease application, as well as lease negotiations. The chapter concludes by discussing the three essential topics of contract management, start of lease term activities, and applicable federal and state laws.

By the end of this chapter, you should have an understanding of residential leasing and can decide if this is something you want to pursue as a career.

Chapter Outline

Defining the Terms of the Lease

Commission to Agent(s)

Marketing a Property for Lease

Showing the Property

Tenant Screening

The Lease Application

Reading a Typical Lease Application

Identifying Red Flags on Lease Applications

Common Problems with Lease Applications

Lease Application Denial Letter

Lease Terms

Lease Negotiations

Lease Contract Management

Start of Lease Term

Federal and State Laws

About Residential Leasing

Leasing a residential property (condos, apartments, or single-family homes) includes the following seven steps. You and the landlord should first define the lease terms, then market the property for lease, show the property to prospective tenants, screen the tenants, negotiate the lease, and finally, manage the lease terms. These steps are discussed in detail in the following sections.

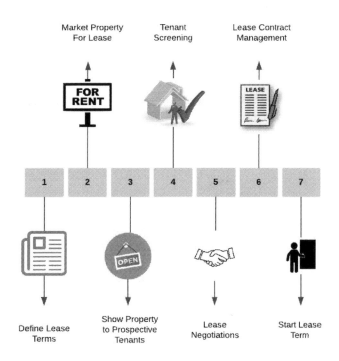

Figure 42 - The Residential Leasing Process

Defining the Terms of the Lease

You should provide the landlord with a valuation. The valuation should include comparables. Ideally, you should provide the owner with details of each property leased within the past three months within a quarter of a mile of the subject property. If there are insufficient comparables, you should expand the search for comparables to 6 months and/or 0.5 miles.

Work with the landlord to define the following lease terms:

- Monthly Rent Amount (based on the comparables)
- Deposit Amount
- Is water included or excluded?
- Is gas included, excluded, or not applicable?
- Is electricity included or excluded?
- Is yard maintenance service included or excluded?

- Are pets allowed? Cats? Dogs? Small only? Any size?
- If there is an HOA, does the tenant pay the HOA fee? What is included?

Commission to Agent(s)

You should define the commission payable to you. Typically in Los Angeles County, the commission can be either 5% or 6% for residential transactions. The commission should be split between the agent representing the buyer and the agent representing the seller. It is also reasonable to offer a minimum commission if this is a low valued/short term lease.

Marketing a Property for Lease

You will market the property for lease based on the above-proposed terms of a lease. Your marketing efforts should aim at a minimum to include:

- Photos and videos created by a professional photographer.
- A virtual 3D tour
- Placing the property on the local MLS
- Advertising the property on Apartments.com
- Placing a For Lease sign (if permitted)
- Advertising the property on Craigslist.com
- Advertising the property on Social Media

For luxury properties, a dedicated website to market the property is suggested.

Showing the Property

You should conduct open houses (or virtual open houses). The open houses should be marketed on the MLS as well as social media.

You should also allow for private showings upon request.

Tenant Screening

Screening candidate tenants is one of the essential parts of the leasing process. It helps evaluate the risk and helps choose the best quality tenants from the various applicants. Ensuring good quality tenants can mean increased revenue. It also enhances the reputation of a property. Good tenants stay longer, reduce periods of vacancy, which increases revenues, and reduces stress for property owners and managers.

Every applicant must be treated equally in the screening process. Always follow established procedures and ask for identification first.

Ideally, you want a tenant with a stable job, good credit history, and no criminal record. You want the tenant to afford the rent and want them to stay at the property for the duration you have it available for lease.

You should use a reputable online screening service that will run each prospect's credit report and background check and allow the prospects to upload all relevant documents for your review.

A prospective tenant that is not willing to register and pay for such services is not serious. This allows you to eliminate some candidates.

Once the landlord reviews the tenant's package you provided them, they can request additional documentation if the package is not complete or reject the prospective tenant based on the partial package.

Once the package is complete, you should conduct a comprehensive review of the package and interview the candidate.

You should report the outcome of the interview with the landlord and make a recommendation. You can then ask the landlord if they wish to proceed to meet the candidate tenant at the property before moving to the contract stage or if they wish to pass.

The Lease Application

The lease application presents a tenant's rental history. Proper handling of a lease application is needed to protect your business, yourself, and your reputation.

You should use a lease application from a reputable source, know what information to collect, learn how to interpret the information you collect, know how to verify the information, look out for red flags, understand the laws related to residential leasing, and avoid actions that may be discriminatory.

Reading a Typical Lease Application

You need to know how to read, understand, and use the lease application to achieve your leasing goals.

Many agents, landlords, and property managers take the easy way out by just glancing at the income listed and then running a credit report. Finding the right tenant requires a thorough analysis.

A typical lease application includes personal information, property details, residence history, employment, income information, financial information, and information about pets and vehicles (see Figure 43). These are discussed in the following sections.

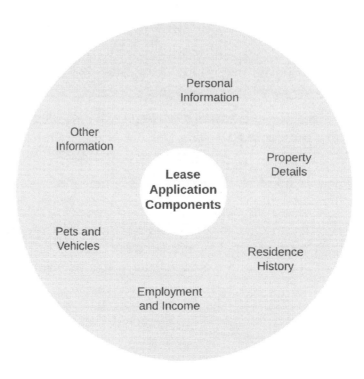

Figure 43 - Lease Application Components

Personal Information

Personal information is needed to verify the identity of the individuals applying to lease the property and getting an idea of who is applying. You or the landlord should gather some essential information to keep on file if you want to contact the applicant or file an unlawful detainer down the road.

Name - Applicants will provide their first, middle, and last names.

Some applicants with an unfavorable lease history may pretend to be someone else who has a better track record. Ensure that the name on the application matches the name provided on any government-issued ID you collect. Online systems provide automatic identity verification for each screening report.

When screening applicants, make sure the name provided is their legal name. Also, maintaining correct names for all tenants can help you keep tenants accountable if there are any issues later on that require an eviction or collections.

Social Security Number - It is possible to collect this on a standard lease application. However, some suggest you do not require a social security number on a lease application. Many agents and property managers require an SSN or even reject applicants who do not provide one.

Doing this may be interpreted as discriminating against applicants based on their national origin, a federally protected class. Such action can result in a substantial fine.

You do not need an SSN to run tenant screening reports! Online tenant screening systems provide full tenant screening reports that do not require the applicant's SSN.

If you feel that you must have an SSN to keep on file for tenants, you should consider asking for the SSN during the lease signing process and not during the lease application process.

Other occupants - Applicants should always list the other individuals who will occupy the unit. It is essential to know exactly who will be living there. Make sure you are collecting complete information from all adult occupants. With that information, you can determine if the applicant(s) will be a good fit for the property,

Let us look at two scenarios:

A couple applies. They specify that the other occupants are their ten children and four parents. You can factor this into your decision-making process and determine if your property's size can accommodate the total number of occupants.

An individual applies. In the "Other Occupants" section, another individual is listed who is over 18 years of age. You should make sure that the other occupant applies and is screened separately as well.

Phone Numbers – Beneficial to have in case you need to ask any follow-up questions during your screening process. You can use them to get in touch with tenants if you need to down the road, for example, to track down those who have not paid rent.

Date of Birth - Helps you verify the candidate's identity. Make sure that the date of birth matches with any identification provided by an applicant. Some screening reports may also provide the date of birth for the applicant, in which case you can double-check the information to make sure everything matches. The date of birth also lets you determine whether or not an occupant needs to complete an application. For example, you can not hold minors responsible for rent, so you would not screen them.

Age is a protected class, so you cannot use age as a basis for legally denying an applicant. Developing and applying screening criteria equally to all applicants helps protect you if you ask for the date of birth on your lease application.

Government-Issued Identification - Most lease applications request the applicant to include information related to government-issued identification (ID type, ID number, issuing government agency, and expiration date). You should make sure that all of the information matches to ensure there is no misrepresentation.

Property Details

Information about the property you are leasing should be included on a lease application to ensure you are on the same page with the applicant(s). It also helps you keep applications organized in case you are working with multiple vacancies simultaneously.

The property address, rent amount, and the security deposit should be included. This reminds the applicant(s) what you are asking for and saves everyone's time if the amounts exceed the applicant's budget.

Residence History

Reviewing an applicant's residence history is essential to the decision you will make about each applicant. It includes the following:

Current Residence - An applicant's current residence is the first step, looking back at the residence history.

Residence Type - The applicant can indicate whether they are currently living in a leased unit or in a property they own. If an applicant currently lives in a leased unit, you can contact the current landlord and confirm move-in/move-out dates. For applicants who live in a property they own, find out why they want to move into the leased property.

Current address – Using the current address, you can verify that you are speaking with the actual landlord. Screening reports usually have the address history, so you can check to see that the lease application's address matches the landlord reference check and the address history on the screening reports. By comparing, you can identify red flags on a lease application.

Move-in / move-out dates – Used for cross-referencing when contacting the landlord. A large, unexplained gap in residence can indicate that the applicant is trying to hide a negative lease experience with a previous landlord. You should make sure an applicant's residence history is reported.

Landlord name and contact information – It is crucial to contact landlord references to learn more about the applicant and verify lease history. Missing the landlord's name and contact information is a big red flag.

An applicant may list a friend or relative instead of the actual landlord. One thing you can do when you call the landlord is not to provide the landlord with any of the information you are asking about. Let the landlord provide you the detail about the property address, rent amount, and move-in dates. An actual landlord will be able to provide you with this information, so you can quickly tell if something unethical is happening.

Reason for moving out –Reasonable responses include relocating for work or looking for a larger place. Leaving this field blank is a red flag. Moving out due to eviction is another red flag.

Check the reason for moving out when you contact references. For example, if the applicant lists they are moving for a new job, you should be able to contact the current and previous employers to verify this information.

Previous Residence(s) - It is critical to contact previous landlords. The current landlord might not tell the whole truth about a bad tenant because they may just want to get rid of the tenant. Previous landlords have no reason to hide such information.

Employment and Income Information

You want to know if the applicant makes enough monthly income to cover the rent and other living expenses. You also want to make sure that the source of income is reasonably stable.

Employer information includes the employer name, address, supervisor/HR manager name. Use this information to perform an employment verification. You should gather proof of income from the applicant (pay stubs, W-2s) and ensure that the employer information matches up. When you contact the employer, have them verify all the information provided by the applicant. Any inconsistencies between the employer and the lease application should be investigated.

By law, you cannot discriminate against the type of income, so it's essential to account for the various types of income provided.

When defining your tenant screening criteria, specify a minimum rent to income ratio you are comfortable with (a typical rent to income ratio is 30%).

Pets and Vehicles

Help make sure there is a good fit between the applicant and your policies. For instance, if you only have one available parking space for the property you are renting, and you see two vehicles listed on the lease application, you may want to contact the applicant to discuss this before moving further with the application.

This section of the lease application serves as a reference later. For example, if an applicant indicates one dog on their application, but you later find out that the tenant has six dogs, you will have the lease application to reference for any action you might need to take.

Some applicants may have a service animal or an emotional support animal. It may appear discriminatory to reject applicants because they have such an animal, even with a no-pets policy in place.

Additional Information

Most lease applications have a miscellaneous section, which may include questions about evictions, bankruptcies, and felony convictions.

These questions can also help pre-screen applicants before you move forward. You can usually verify the answers provided by running tenant screening reports on the applicant.

Identifying Red Flags on Lease Applications

Aside from the obvious indicators such as low credit score and insufficient income, there are other details on a lease application that may point to an unqualified tenant. Identifying these will help you minimize problems down the road.

Encountering any of the following red flags requires additional research for disqualification:

- Contact information not provided for current/previous landlord
- Credit report provided by the applicant – and applicant is not willing to have you run a report
- Currently unemployed and/or no income
- Frequent changes of residence
- Income is unverifiable
- Incomplete information provided
- Information provided does not match screening reports
- The applicant is breaking the lease with their current landlord
- The applicant is in a rush

Common Problems with Lease Applications

The tenant application form you use is the basis of your tenant screening process. With a thorough lease application, you reduce your legal risk and maximize your chances of finding a good tenant.

More and more brokerages use online screening services. These services allow the applicants to apply online (they pay for the service). The applicants upload documents, and the service runs all the checks. You then review all materials and request any information and/or documents that may be missing. Next, you proceed to discuss the applicants' qualifications with the owner.

Lease Application Denial Letter

Denying applicants is unavoidable when handling properties for lease.

It is crucial to ensure you treat applicants fairly and not engage in any discriminatory practices when denying an applicant. Common reasons to deny lease applicants:

- Co-applicant/guarantor was denied
- Credit score or credit report
- Income-to-rent ratio
- Incomplete lease application or misrepresentation on the application
- Unfavorable residence history
- Unverifiable income

You need to make sure you are applying the same denial criteria equally to all applicants. It is best to record your acceptance/rejection ranges for each factor you will be evaluating.

Evaluate applicants in the order in which you receive their information. When you receive a completed application package from an applicant, you should document the time you received it and apply your rejection policy before moving on to the next person who applies. You would ideally accept the first applicant that meets your minimum criteria and stop looking at additional applicants.

Letting applicants know when they are rejected is a critical step required to minimize legal issues. According to the Fair Credit Reporting Act (FCRA), you must provide a lease application denial letter if you reject an applicant based in whole or in part on any consumer reports. That is, if a credit report, credit score, background, or eviction report is factored into your rejection decision, then you must notify the applicant.

Lease Terms

A typical residential lease includes the following terms/clauses (see Figure 44):

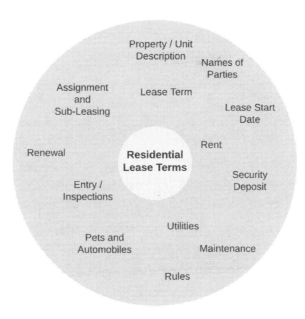

Figure 44 - Typical Residential Lease Terms

- **Property / Unit description** – address and property condition (attach a walkthrough form)
- **Names of parties** - landlord / tenant(s), and possibly co-signers (e.g. parents of university students)
- **Lease term** – Typically one year term
- **Lease start date**
- **Rent** – amount and due dates
- **Security deposit** – in the event of damages to the unit

- **Utilities** – which party pays for what
- **Maintenance** – which party pays for what
- **Rules** – of the building, HOA, governing the tenant's use of the unit and common areas
- **Pets and Automobiles** – types of pets, number of pets, number of automobile parking spots, guest parking
- **Entry / Inspections** – emergency entry, notice ahead of an inspection
- **Renewal** – Notice to be provided before the renewal date, including changes to rent
- **Assignment and Sub-Leasing**
- **Defects** – disclose any known defects

Lease Negotiations

The prospective tenant may agree to all of your proposed terms for the lease, or they may not. The prospective tenant should be aware of the lease terms advertised but may counter with their terms. You should shield the owner from direct contact by the tenant at this stage.

Terms that may be negotiated include:

- Monthly rent amount
- Deposit amount
- Move-in date
- Term of lease
- Who pays for utilities and services

You should provide the property owner with the terms requested and make a recommendation to accept or suggestions on how to counter each term. You should also explain to the property owner your reasoning for the proposed response.

Once the property owner approves the counter terms, you will take them to the prospective tenant. The process may iterate several times until reaching an agreement or realizing an agreement can not be reached.

Lease Contract Management

You can use the Residential Lease or Month-to-Month Lease Agreement (C.A.R. Form LR). You should use an electronic signature service such as DocuSign.com to have the property owner and the tenant(s) sign the lease.

Start of Lease Term

The tenant can either mail you the first month's rent plus deposit or meet you or the landlord at the property and provided it to you at the time of the final walkthrough. Once the walkthrough has been completed, and the tenant has provided payment, keys to the property should be provided to the tenant. You should receive the commission payment and, in turn, issue a check to the tenant's agent if there was one.

Federal and State Laws

You should be aware of several federal and state laws and operate, having them in mind. They include:

- Antitrust Laws
- Megan's Law
- Lead-Based Paint Hazard Reduction Act
- Fair Housing Act
- Americans with Disabilities Act (ADA)
- Equal Credit Opportunity Act (ECOA)
- Fair Credit Reporting Act (FCRA)
- Servicemembers Civil Relief Act (SCRA)

Chapter 18 - Commercial Leasing

Chapter Overview

Chapter 18 looks at some of what commercial leasing agents do. It starts with reviewing the components of a commercial leasing application package and then looks at such applications' review process.

The chapter proceeds to survey the different types of commercial leases and the key terms included in them.

By the end of this chapter, you should have a basic understanding of commercial leasing and can decide if this is something you want to pursue as a career.

Chapter Outline

Components of a Commercial Leasing Application Package

Application Review

Types of Commercial Leases

Typical Terms of Commercial Leases

About Commercial Leasing

Commercial tenant applications are more complex than residential ones. They require information about the business and the individual(s) overseeing the business and/or looking to lease on its behalf.

Components of a Commercial Leasing Application Package

Commercial applications typically require:

- Description of the business / how it operates
- Lease signer's name, role in the business (Owner, CEO, etc.)
- Owners'/Management names, contact information, and biographies
- Financials of the business
- Planned improvements (if any) to the space being leased
- Commercial lease history: names and contact information of past landlords

A typical package includes the application as well as a combination of some or all of the following documents:

- Business Plan
- Franchise Agreement
- Organizing documents (Articles of Incorporation, LLC Agreement, etc.)
- Personal financial statement
- Budget
- Profit and Loss Statement
- Resumes of key individuals
- Tax returns (corporate and / or personal)
- IDs of the individuals that will sign the lease

Application Review

Small and medium-sized business owners are often required to guarantee the lease personally. Screening of the individuals signing the lease, business owners, and/or top management may be necessary once you determine that the business may be a fit for the property you are leasing. You should speak with the applicant(s), owners and/or management, as well as past landlords.

You should review financials to make sure they indicate a stable or growing business, with a realistic multi-year business plan and budget. You should also make sure the management has the experience to run this business.

For situations where the business and its financials are more complex, you or the landlord might want to have a CPA and/or attorney review the application package as well.

Once a prospective tenant's application package has been reviewed and appears to be a fit, lease negotiations should commence. Lease negotiations involve the review and countering of different lease terms. Types of commercial leases, as well as possible lease terms, are presented next.

Types of Commercial Leases

There are five primary types of commercial leases:

- **Straight Lease/Gross Lease** – tenant pays a fixed amount, and the landlord pays all other expenses.
- **Net Lease** – Tenant pays utilities, taxes, and special assessments in addition to the rent.
- **Net-Net Lease** – Same as a Net lease, but tenant also pays insurance premiums.
- **Triple Net Lease** – Same as Net-Net lease, but tenant also pays for repairs and maintenance.
- **Percentage Lease** – tenant pays fixed lease amount and a percentage of gross income in excess of a minimum amount. This type of lease is commonly used for retail properties.

Typical Terms of Commercial Leases

Typical lease terms/clauses in commercial leases include the following:

- **Legal description** - of the location offered for lease.
- **Existing/proposed floor plans** – of the location.
- **Square footage (SF)**
    - Usable SF – Actual space tenant is to occupy exclusively, without considering the common areas.
    - Rentable SF – Usable SF plus a portion of the building's common areas, such as hallways, lobbies, and storage rooms (inside measurements)
    - Gross SF – The building's entire floor area is measured from the outside.
- **R/U Ratio** – the Rentable SF divided by the Usable SF. The larger this number is, the more the tenant pays towards maintaining common areas (if the price per SF is the same when comparing buildings).
- **Date of possession** – Date when the tenant is provided with the keys and gains access to the property. If there is a period of time for renovations, the possession date is prior to the lease start date.
- **Lease start date** – Date when the tenant can move. If there is a significant build-out or remodel, the lease start date may be uncertain and therefore specified as "X days after build-out (or remodel) is complete."
- **Tenant Improvement Allowance (TIA)** – Amount of money that a landlord is willing to provide to the tenant to cover all or a portion of the build-out costs of a tenant's space.
- **Lease Term** - The more customized the build-out, the longer the term is likely to be.
    - Office lease – Typically 3-5 year term
    - General Retail – 3-5 year term
    - Restaurants – 10 or more year terms
    - Anchor tenants – 20 or more year terms

There are additional terms specific to different types of commercial properties outside the scope of this chapter that you should be familiar with if you plan to focus on commercial leasing. For example:

- **Office leasing** - often also considers issues such as building security, tenant mix, future employee growth accommodation, use restrictions
- **Retail leasing** - rent-to-sales ratio, base rent, percentage rent, breakpoints, recapture, tenant operating hours, signage and advertising, use restrictions
- **Industrial leasing** - use restrictions, inspections, specialized insurance, environmental issues

Chapter 19 - Real Estate Investing

Chapter Overview

Chapter 19 looks at what real estate investors need to know and what they might do. It starts with a look at the yield, safety, and liquidity of real estate investments. It proceeds to discuss the advantages and disadvantages of investing in real estate.

The chapter concludes with a look at different real estate investment strategies.

By the end of this chapter, you should have a basic understanding of real estate investing and can decide if this is something you want to pursue as a career. Some real estate agents start their careers focused on helping investors, and then once they accumulate some money, they start investing themselves.

Chapter Outline

About the yield of Real Estate Investments

About the Safety of Real Estate Investments

About the Liquidity of Real Estate Investments

Advantages of Investing in Real Estate

Disadvantages of Investing in Real Estate

Real Estate Investment Strategies

Selecting an Agent to Help You with Real Estate Acquisitions

About Investing in Real Estate

You can invest in stocks, bonds, CDs, commodities, etc. You can also invest in residential and/or commercial real estate. Many financial advisors would tell you it is best to diversify. Many investors invest in commercial and/or real estate as part of your diversified investment portfolio. Other investors focus strictly on commercial and/or residential real estate.

Different types of investments generate different types of returns. The return on real estate investment takes the form of rents, additional income (for example, building advertisement), as well as an appreciation of the value of the asset (see Figure 45).

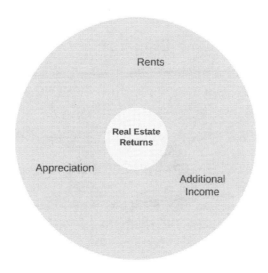

Figure 45 - Types of Real Estate Returns

Investors in real estate look at three key characteristics: Yield, Safety, and Liquidity (see Figure 46). These characteristics are discussed briefly next.

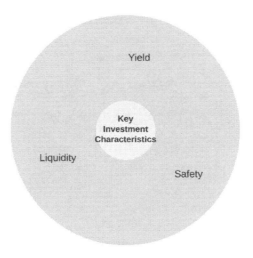

Figure 46 - Key Investment Characteristics

About the Yield of Real Estate Investments

Yield is the rate of return on the investment. Yield related rules include:

- A risky real estate investment with a low yield is not of interest to many investors.
- The riskier the real estate investment, the higher the yield needs to be to attract the investors.
- Given the same risk, an investor is likely to pick the real estate investment with a higher yield.
- Investors expect higher yields on longer-term investments as compensation for having their capital tied up for more extended periods.

About the Safety of Real Estate Investments

A safer investment is one where an investor has a lower risk of losing their money. Some investors prefer safer investments, even if the yield is lower. Others prefer higher yield and will accept the risk that goes with it.

Real Estate assets are considered one of the safest types of investments.

About the Liquidity of Real Estate Investments

A liquid investment is one that can be converted to cash quickly. Real estate assets are one of the least liquid types of assets. Typically it can take 30-60 days to sell an asset. If the asset is unique, it may take a much longer time to sell an asset, and if money is needed fast, the property might need to be sold below market value.

Advantages of Investing in Real Estate

There are four primary advantages to investing in real estate (see Figure 47):

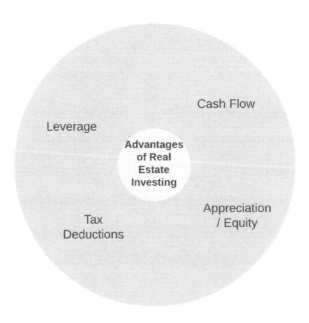

Figure 47 - Advantages of Investing in Real Estate

- **Cash flow** – the typical outcome from owning a property and leasing it to tenants for monthly income.
- **Appreciation and equity** – real estate in much of the US has shown an increase in value over time. As a property's value increases, so should your equity unless you refinance to cash out.
- **Tax Deductions** – depreciation, mortgage interest, and some operating expenses can be used as tax deductions.
- **Leverage** – using borrowed money (mortgage) to make money.

Disadvantages of Investing in Real Estate

There are five disadvantages to investing in real estate (see Figure 48):

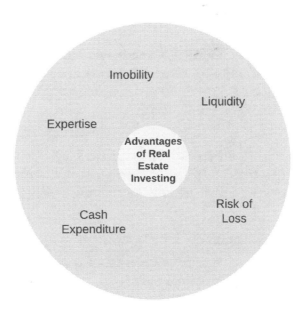

Figure 48 - Disadvantages of Investing in Real Estate

- **Liquidity** – Real estate is not a very liquid asset, as discussed earlier.
- **Risk of Loss** – in the event of a downturn when tenant(s) stop paying rent or real estate values fall substantially.
- **Cash Expenditure** – investing in real estate may require a significant amount of money as a down payment (in some parts of the country).
- **Expertise** – need to have the right agent that can identify the best deal possible for a given situation.

- **Immobility** – If a neighborhood starts to decline, your client's investment can not be physically moved. It is crucial to utilize an agent who knows how to determine long term prospects of various neighborhoods through analysis to identify where you may wish to invest on behalf of your client. "Local experts" are often biased and tell you that their neighborhoods are good to invest in.

Real Estate Investment Strategies

Properties in high priced and appreciating markets do well using the short term buy and hold strategy, where properties for lease are owned for a short period, and during that time, value is added. Some of the ways value can be added are renovating and increasing rents, and decreasing expenses.

Another short-term strategy is to fix and flip a home. You can identify fixer opportunities and experienced and reputable vendors to have the property renovated. Permits should be obtained for all work that requires permits.

You can then sell the property at a profit. Not every "fixer" property is a good candidate for this strategy. This requires a cost/benefit analysis to determine if and what level of profits to expect from a renovation.

Another investment strategy consists of purchasing a fixer, adding value, and leasing it. Some investors use this first property as leverage to purchase their next property, and so on. For example, in Los Angeles County, there are over 400 investors that own between 10 and 50 single-family homes.

Some investors start by purchasing a turnkey vacant rental property, lease it, and generate income while waiting for its value to appreciate. Other investors identify commercial properties with high vacancy rates. They replace the property management company, upgrade the building(s) and other structure(s) if necessary, increase rents, sell it, or keep it in their portfolios.

Some investors keep their portfolios for years and eventually sell them. Others pass their portfolios to their children.

If you have any ideas for improvement of this book please email me at david@GeffenRealEstate.com or text me at 310-433-0694

If you enjoyed this book, please consider posting a review. Even if it's only a few sentences, it would be a huge help. Thank you.

Made in the USA
Las Vegas, NV
10 August 2022